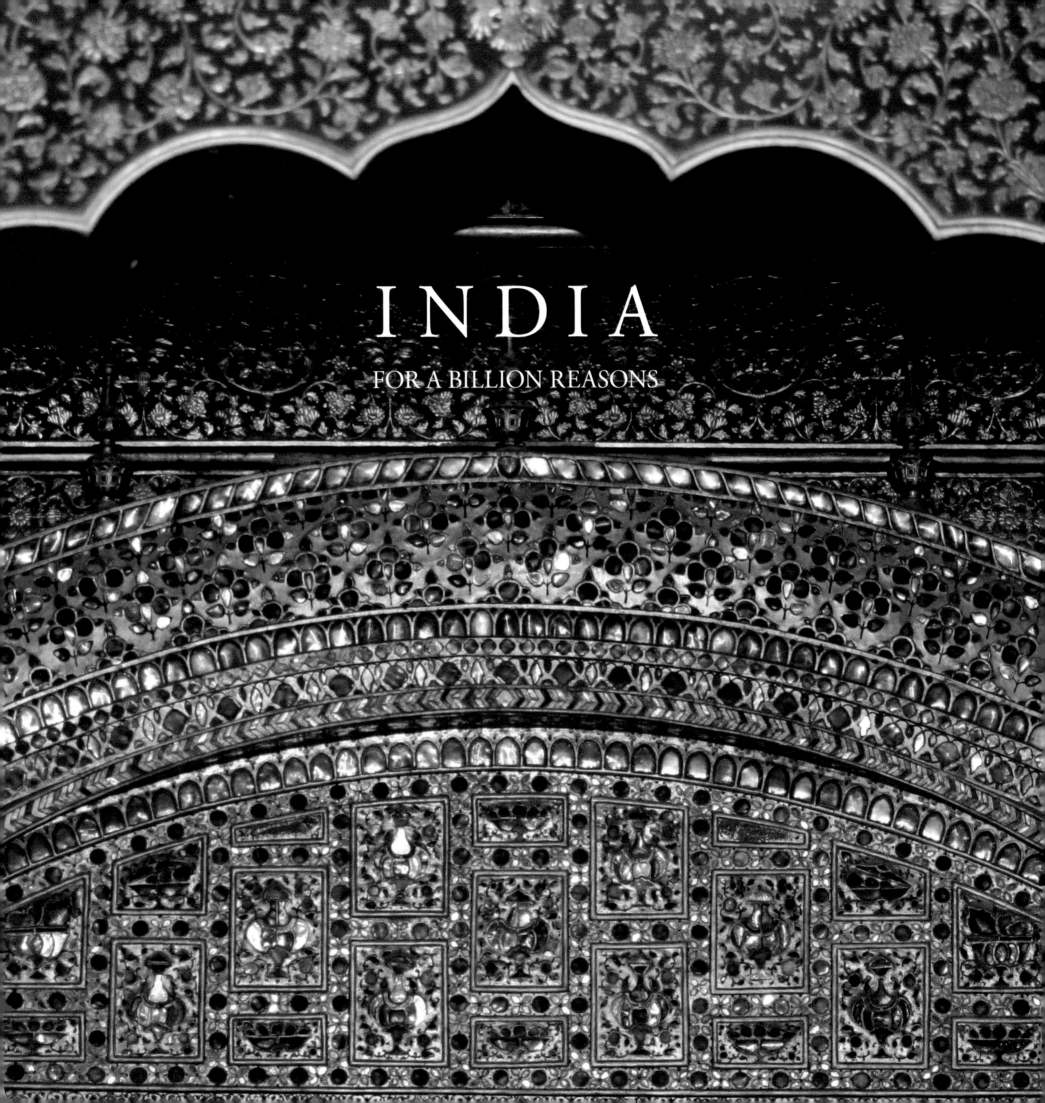

INDIA

FOR A BILLION REASONS

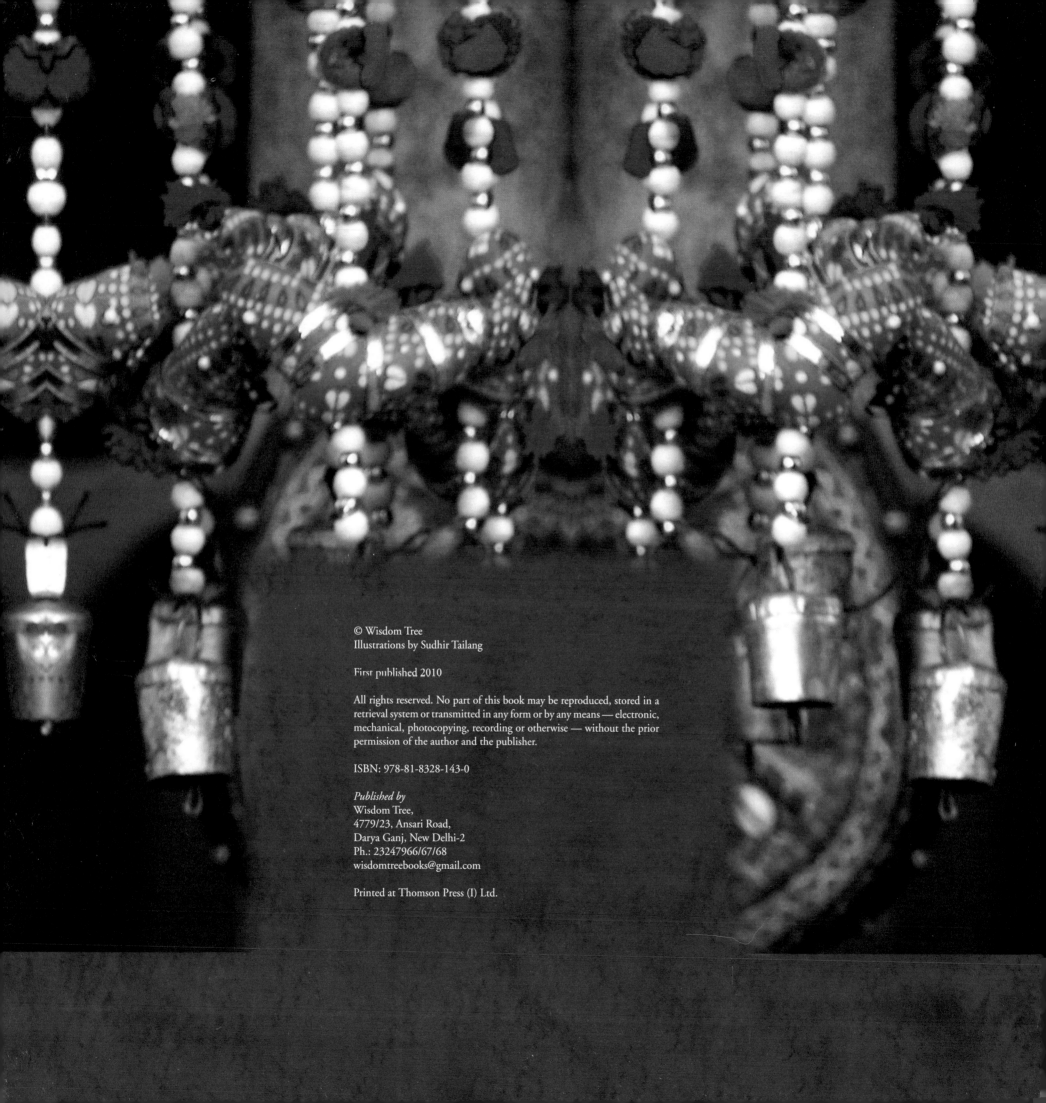

ISBN: 978-81-8328-143-0

Published by
Wisdom Tree,
4779/23, Ansari Road,
Darya Ganj, New Delhi-2
Ph.: 23247966/67/68
wisdomtreebooks@gmail.com

Printed at Thomson Press (I) Ltd.

I N D I A

for

A BILLION REASONS

wisdom
tree

Contents

The Sum of Its Parts.. 1

Pulse and Impulse: Rhythmic Journeys Through the Dances of India........................ 13

Art from India... 33

The Living Crafts of India: Unbroken Continuities.. 45

Why Hollywood is Romancing Bollywood.. 59

Contemporary Indian Literature.. 73

Curried Away... 87

State of Indian Sports: A Glass Half Empty or Half Full.. 113

The Indian Polity.. 133

India's Economic Tryst with Destiny... 147

The Press in India... 161

The Ascent to Modernity.. 175

What India Means to Me.. 195

Glossary... 203

Photograph Credits... 205

The Sum of Its Parts

Atri Bhattacharya

*A*rsalan Meyehane. The sign at the *Cicek Pasaj* (Flower Lane) in Istanbul stopped me dead in my tracks. Not just because it appeared at the end of a long thirst-inducing walk. Not just because, thanks to Kemal Pasha and his proscription of Arabic script, it was in Roman letters. What struck me was the echo of India in this city on the cusp of two continents. *Meyehane* or bar is almost exactly the same as *maikhana* – that staple of poor Urdu *shayari*. And Arsalan is one of *The Wife's* favourite restaurants back in Kolkata. It set me to deep thoughts about how the world is reflected in India. I retired to the *meyehane* to sluice my mental processes with *raqi* (which, alas, has no counterpart in India).

Minor irrigation yielded a flood of impressions. Travelling the world after three decades of exploring India, yields a continuous state of déjà vu. In the alleys of Aleppo, cobbled and cloistered, sometimes almost claustrophobic, I thought, "I have been here before." *Shall I say I have gone at dusk through narrow streets …* That would be Varanasi, the lanes of Godhaulia that rise and fall and eddy into uneven stairs, or break into sudden effusions of multicoloured shops and garish lights. Or the winding lanes in Lisbon's Alfama, where, in a yellow tram car hurtling between shop fronts close enough to touch, I found echoes of Surya Sen Street in Calcutta (now Kolkata). The Edwardian facades of old Calcutta came to mind again, and the Indo-Saracenic architecture of south Bombay (now Mumbai), on a walk that took me down Piccadilly and up Oxford Street. A sleepy courtyard in Damascus, arches and pillars around a cracked pavement gently heaving like a summer sea, the dome of a mosque rising beyond the outer wall, could just as well have been in Lucknow. Near Sao Paulo, a church gleaming white against a hillside riotously green — comes to life from a photograph taken in the late afternoon sun near Benaulim in Goa. From the air force observation post on Laitkor Peak in Shillong, green meadows roll towards a hilly horizon, blurring into memories of a drive from Lancaster to the Lake District. Louvred windows look out on the lanes in Pudducherry that run towards the sea, with street signs still posted in French.

(Pages vi – vii) Bhandasar Temple, Bikaner — India's temples are exemplary of her elaborate and decorative architecture.

A local man traces the mystic dunes of Thar, Jaisalmer.

The trademark yellow Kolkata taxi in front of Victoria Memorial in Kolkata.

Kipling's Kim, protagonist of one of the greatest road novels, is a "little friend of all the world." How apt for a book that is still one of the best accounts of India, for India itself is a little picture of "all the world." Three thousand years, waves of invaders, ripples of traders and millennia of assimilation; Greeks, Turks, Persians, the descendants of the Mongols, Portuguese, French and finally the British; a patchwork quilt of history that comes to life through the senses. A snatch of song in a *nargileh* bar that sounds eerily like Bangla *adhunik* — the same cadences, a similar tune, even words that echo my mother tongue. Curry and rice from a roadside stall in Bangkok, the aroma and the feel of comfort — taking one back to late winter nights at Khyber near the Delhi Ridge. The sudden explosion of a laugh in a smoky room, and the latticework above the arched doorway suddenly turns into Café Britannia near Ballard Pier in Mumbai.

The downside of the Indian experience is that it leaves us a little jaded for the rest of the world. James Elroy Flecker's lush verse drove me to the gates of Damascus. Only to leave me disappointed. Because I have seen the Buland Darwaza in Fatehpur Sikri and there can be no comparison. The giant dome of the Hagia Sofia is slightly less awe-inspiring when one has seen the Gol Gumbaz in Bijapur. Everywhere one goes, one has to fight the inner voice of Mark Twain's hayseed that had 'been there and seen that'.

It's not just the diversity in the culture, nor even the weight of 5000 years of history. The sheer physical differences are sometimes difficult to comprehend. In the 50°C summers of Vizag or Bhopal, birds drop dead from the sky, at the same time soldiers in the upper reaches of Leh need fuel to melt their drinking water. Every school-going child in India is aware of the contrasts from west to east, the stretches of the Thar desert (a friend from Bikaner told me he had never seen rain till he was four!) and the sodden slopes of Cherrapunji. The Himalayas, which beggar description even when seen from a hundred miles away, or from a porthole at 38,000 feet. The festering mangrove swamps of the Sundarbans, heavy with tropic heat and the ever-present terror of the Royal Bengal Tiger. The boulder-stippled, sinewy ravines of the Seonee River in India's

heartland, flowing through the tawny meadows and shape-shifting trees of Pench. The Sergio Leone landscapes of the Rann of Kutch and the Victorian propriety of pensioners' colonies in Mashobra.

On the west bank of the Hooghly in West Bengal, a thirty kilometre stretch is a lesson in the history of colonisation. Bandel Church was built in thanksgiving by a shipwrecked Portuguese trader, and the Marthomite cross is testimony to its origins. Chinsurah, farther down the river, was a trading post for the Dutch. Some of the older residents of Chandannagar, just south of Chinsurah, still hold French citizenship and receive pensions from the French government. The Institut de Chandernagore on the Strand road still runs classes in French and has a library of books on France. More relevant, perhaps, is the institution of Lords Bakery, which may be the only authentic *boulangerie* within a thousand miles. Travelling farther down, Rishra, once a German trading station and indigo factory, still has a neighbourhood called Alemaanpara. Srirampur was Frederiksnagar under the Danish East India Company, before the arrival of the two Williams, Carey and Ward. By the middle of the nineteenth century all these towns were under the rule of the Viceroy of Her Majesty's Government in India. All except Chandannagar, which remained a French territory until ceded to India in February 1951. This anomalous enclave also played a part in India's freedom movement — as French territory, it was a haven for the young revolutionaries pursued by the British in India. Memories of five countries from the continent, all to be swamped by a sixth.

Bloodlines of the earliest recorded invaders live on in remote pockets of the Himalayan foothills. The village of Malana in Himachal Pradesh is closed to outsiders. The locals claim descent from Greek armies (more probably Seleucus' men than Alexander's) and have their own distinct religion. The language of the Drukpa, a polyandrous tribe in Ladakh, is different from the regions surrounding them, and it is surmised that they too (like the inhabitants of Nuristan across the border, famously celebrated in Hollywood film *The Man who would be King*) descended from some wandering arm of Greek forces. Ladakh itself, marked with *chortens*, fed on *thukpa* and *tsampa*, is a little echo of Tibet. In the eighties, the Sports Authority of India picked boys from the obscure Siddhi tribe in Andhra Pradesh to train them as long distance runners.

It turned out that they were relying on genetics, because the Siddhis are supposed to be descendants of Ethiopian warriors brought over by the Nawabs of Hyderabad.

They were all here once. India holds them still.

It takes more than a journey to comprehend this country. The British had this tradition at the turn of the last century, the Grand Tour. The closest Indian equivalent may be in the civil services, where officers in training are sent around the country on *Bharat Darshan* (tour of India). In the year that I joined the civil service, possibly like every other year, everybody wanted to go to Goa. Our group went instead to Jammu and Gujarat, to Bombay and to Bangalore (now Bangaluru). We watched sunset over the Arabian Sea from the deck of a frigate, tiptoed down border trails in Akhnoor in the dark before dawn, ate Vadilal ice creams and thalis beside the highway near Ahmedabad. For thirty days, the sights of India washed over us in waves. At the end of it all, we listed all the places we hadn't visited and the sights we hadn't seen even in the states we passed through — the step wells of Gujarat, the mustard fields of Punjab, the brooding citadels of Mandu and Orchha, the ruins of Hampi. Thirty days were never enough to see a tenth of this bewildering variety.

We did, however, get a feel of the people. Because we rode the rails. Through long nights and longer days, lulled by the rattle of wheels, we spoke to people. To Indians. A studious Sikh accountant from Ludhiana, so different from the stereotype of the bluff Sardar. A group of feisty old ladies from Surat, travelling down to Bombay to run a sale. The homesick young sailor going up from Vishakhapatnam to Kanpur, looking forward to his mother's cooking. In hindsight, that young man personified two of the strands that bind together this crazy sprawl. First, the armed forces, where discipline and uniformity blur the differences between regions and races. Second, the railways, that uniquely Indian melting pot where the diverse ingredients are tossed together.

Konkan railway track, Mangalore to Goa — Indian railways forms the backbone of the country and offers an opportunity to befriend its varied cultures.

The iron horse had more than an economic impact on the process of 'nation-building'. Besides opening up the Indian hinterland to trade, the railways broke down divisions in society and opened up their minds. An aphroism from nineteenth century Bengal has survived — *Jaat bhanglo teen Sen — Keshob Sen, Wil-sen aar ishtisen.* Loosely translated, three Sens demolished the barriers of caste — Keshob Sen (the Brahmo reformer), Wilson's Hotel in Calcutta where people dined together regardless of their caste and the *ishtisen* or railway station, where people were thrown together in the adventure of travel. Travellers from Theroux to Iyer have vouched that a second-class railway carriage on a long journey is the best way to understand the soul of India. Also, to share biographies and genealogies, prepare strategies for the sowing season and the stock market, plan a holiday with (recent) strangers who are suddenly good friends and find a suitable boy for the neighbour's distressingly modern daughter.

A railway carriage would also be the best place to face the stereotyping that moulds regional identities. The burly Sikh, bearded and turbaned, ever-ready to break into an energetic *bhangra* after a meal of *tann-ddoori chik-ken*, good-humoured and good-hearted and typecast as the 'jolly good fellow'. The fish-eating, emotional, argumentative Bengali, wordy and quick-tempered but a physical coward. The Gujarati moneybags who would sell their family for a profit. The "North-Eastern" student, a catch-all categorisation that ignores the distinctions between the Manipuri Bishnupriya and the Baptist from Mizoram, let alone the differences between the sixteen major tribes and sixty-four sub-tribes of Nagaland. Is this merely an attempt to fit people into categories, or is it symptomatic of the emphasis on sub-regional identities? Shall we see in India a replay of what is happening in Georgia and in Moldova, a continuous process of differentiation and division?

My generation was fed the line of 'unity in diversity' long before 'India shining' became a catchphrase. I have problems with both. The diversity is self-evident, but the unity seems more tenuous with each passing year. Some years ago I was in Manipur on government work and became used to the term "you Indians". Even

"going to India". It stirred déjà vu. Then I remembered Kashmir in 1990. These words and the attitude were chilling echoes of a horrific fortnight in Srinagar all those years ago. That's some unity. Consider the Jarawa tribesman in the Andaman Islands. He may not even *know* about India. His home is closer to Thailand than to the Indian mainland. In case I've failed to get the point across, the idea of 'India united' seems to fall well short of a consensus.

It's some kind of miracle that this country still holds together after sixty years.

It's time we realised that there is no such thing as an average Indian.

Because it's time we stopped dealing in stereotypes.

I abhor sounding serious, but the I-word has to come into this somewhere. Identity. What is this Indian identity? What sets me apart from a Bangladeshi or a Pakistani. Precious little, on first examination. Not the national language, Hindi. Not any specific attire. Because our genes are the same, the product of several thousand years in this subcontinental melting pot. We share languages, traditions, cuisine. What then identifies the Indian? We should step outside ourselves for a while to ask, how does the world see Indians? How far are we from the standard shibboleths of mysticism and spirituality and exoticism? In the American media (what, is there any other kind? You mean there are folks out there who don't get Fawx TeeVeeee!) the standard Indian is a nerd. Apu in *The Simpsons* and Raj Patel at Riverdale High. The software geeks who are "taking our jobs to Bangalore". (A skewed perception, since the entire Indian IT workforce is less than 2 million out of a population of 1.13 billion!) In Britain, where Patel may soon be the most common surname (indeed the most common Indian name across the world, from gas stations on mid-Western highways to pulp and insurance magnates in Kenya), India is sadly equated with balti cuisine and Bollywood rap. For the Japanese, India is the cradle of Buddhism. The French made Satyajit Ray a Chevalier of their Legion of Honour. Russia had a long love affair with Indian tea and with Raj Kapoor (though we

Naval display during Paravoor boat race in Cochin.

hear that, of late, Amitabh Bachchan has gained ground). An Indian cannot, reportedly, walk the streets of Cairo without fielding questions on his proximity to Mr B. which is all very well, but is there such a thing as the Indian of the twenty-first century?

Much has been made of Messrs Mittal and Ambani, their pre-eminence among plutocrats and their conspicuous consumption. About how India has 'arrived' because Tata has bought Corus and Jaguar. I agree that this is great news for the urban Indian who reads the financial papers. It means recognition in the international market, it means credibility for our skills and our goods. It means holidays in Latin America, gadgets from Singapore, *mezze* brunches in classy brasseries. And it means sweet damn all to half of India. I could trade it all for evenings like the one I spent in a village in Howrah district back in the nineties. We were visiting learning centres set up under a scheme for functional literacy that employed volunteers. The teacher at the centre was a field labourer who had to drop out of school after fifth grade. This man, with a family of nine to feed, gave hours of his time every evening so that his fellow villagers could learn to read and write. And insisted that we share his dinner before we left. Puffed rice, jaggery cakes and tender coconut water from his own yard. Simple fare that I remember fifteen years later because the unthinking hospitality with which it was offered brooked no refusal.

Hospitality. To paraphrase O. Henry, they will pour their larder into you before they pour their lead. At the height of the Khalistan movement, a friend in the police met some of the most feared insurgents. He shook his head in wonderment as he recounted their first offer — *Duddh shuddh piyo jee*, "Have some hot milk."

Kashmir in 1990, the valley in flames after the shooting of Ishfaq Wani, when a waiter murmured a warning in my ear as we sat down to dinner in the circuit house. But in the same breath, apologised for the meagre fare during the month of fasting. This can border on the farcical. On election duty in Sangroor in Punjab, I found that one candidate's election platform was a large trailer drawn by a Tata Safari, loaded with crates of Solan whiskey and the charred remains of a poultry farm. His appetites were as large as his heart. For every sip he offered, he would take one himself; his day's canvassing ending only when he subsided into the trailer, snoring blissfully. At which point his nephew (on Safari with him, so to speak) would steer homewards. Steer a little erratically, since said nephew shared the family trait of appreciating the simple pleasures (or *plai-years*) of life. When it was pointed out that this amounted to soliciting for votes with promises of gain, the complainant was immediately rebuked and shushed by at least three other candidates, the largest of whom turned to me and said, with a dismissive wave of a huge hand, *Wo koi nahin jee, bacche thodi si jo pee pah lehnde so ki fark painda*, "What does it matter if the boys have a drink or two."

The tradition of hospitality is not limited by India's boundaries. Out on Long Island, the man behind the counter at a Dunkin' Donuts forced cakes and coffee on me, then refused to accept payment because *Apne mulk ke hain aap*, "You are from my country." In Barcelona, I bargained overcurios with a Sindhi shop-lady who would not give an inch or a peso, but pushed two boxes of sweets into my hands as I left, "For your baby". Hospitality. In the simplest form, placing humanity above the self.

Beyond our borders, Indians *are* India. Their clothes, their accents, bindis, spices, worship, top of the class — these are all pixels in the world's reference manual, which is again shaped by the images we propagate. Perhaps the most pervasive images are those in our films. More specifically, Hindi films, because these are most visible to those viewers abroad who do not speak any Indian language. From the loveable layabout in *Awara* through the anti-hero of the seventies, from the unremitting poverty of our early 'art cinema' to the unreal gloss of the Chopra-Johar product, even the perfectly coiffed housewives in our TV serials who don designer chiffons when they go to the kitchen.

Villages with picture-perfect squares conveniently overlooked by impressive *haveli*s. And the strangest part of it all? These places, these characters, exist. You'll come across them in corners of the land untouched by commercialisation. The golden-hearted wino in a palm-shaded bar in the Goan hills. The little shack by a sleepy river and the shade of a bamboo clump. Also the big city industrialist who tries to blight young love. The opulent mansion where *two* staircases lead upstairs from a drawing room larger than Beijing's Bird's Nest stadium.

It's a moot point which is cause and which is effect, which is the original and which is the copy. We can accept that these films have *some* roots in reality — when they're shot on location they must show *some* real places. It's equally true that films create their own reality. Their characters and locales become aspirational for urban India. So it's not only the mannerisms and swagger of the heroes that percolate down to the streets (to be aped by Raju and Rajjak and Rangaswamy). It's also the attire (Oh I *must* have a *lehnga* like the one that Kareena Kapoor wore) and the setting (Oh *jee* I made a fountain in the drawing room like we saw in that *fillum*, so nice only no?). Harshad Mehta reportedly briefed the press from *inside* the confines of a curious desk shaped like a stockade — copied from one used by film villain Ajit. Taking it all in all, 'Incredible India' may be the most truthful India line.

So shall we conclude that India is best reflected in its films? Perhaps not. In fact, certainly not. (If the average urban Indian male adopted Govinda's wardrobe, for example his famous skin-tight red shirt paired with yellow trousers, large numbers of us would have to emigrate.) Mainstream cinema provides, at most, an idea of where India *wants* to be. For where India *is*, I must return to a theme I mentioned earlier. The men in uniform. The character of our armed forces does distinguish India from the neighbouring countries that came into existence at roughly the same time. The Indian Army has remained apolitical for sixty years. Not for us the nights of the generals, the armed coups and the shadow of the gun. Our democracy may be less than perfect, handicapped both by the lack of education among the electorate and the dependence on sub-regional identities. But, it has survived. The very fact that it has survived, however, is a tribute to the common man. And to the soldiers at every level who have never been tempted to pry open the doors of Parliament with their guns. Field Marshal Manekshaw was

Kumbh *mela*, a mass Hindu pilgrimage at Prayag — the holiest of holy confluences.

The modern Indian woman has been moving in step with the times.

arguably India's most famous soldier and certainly the most widely loved. One of the most famous and endearing stories about him is his response when the then Prime Minister asked him whether he was planning a coup against her. His reply was typical of the man. "Madam Prime Minister, I would not prove to be a worthy replacement."

As for unity shall we go over that checklist, then? Physical diversity? Well, our soldiers are everywhere. The snows of Kargil, the tsunami-battered specks of the Andamans, the forests of Arunachal, the deserts of Rajasthan. So represented across the land-check. Ethnic representation? Never in doubt, whether one goes by a list of the Chiefs of the three wings or the composition of a tank squadron in the 61st Cavalry. One Field Marshal from Coorg and one a Parsi born in Amritsar, neither belonging to what one would call a majority ethnic group. Ethnic diversity-check. Immune to the politics of sub-regionalism? Some of the Indian Army's regiments are at least *named* after ethnic groups — the Mahars, the Marathas, the Gurkhas. That's about as far as it goes. They are manned and commanded by men (and lately, by some women as well) from all parts of India. (Yes, even by the wordy, non-martial Bengali). So, ethnic representation-check. United despite the differences of caste and creed? Most certainly. Devoted to the concept of a nation united and sovereign? Next question, please!

So are they most representative of this bewildering land and its chaotic people? Well, taken together, they add up to a whole that is greater than the sum of the parts. Like the country they risk their lives for. I can't think of any better encapsulation of India. Can you?

And if it makes any difference, they're nuts about films and stars as well.

Atri Bhattacharya is a civil servant, who lives behind a keyboard and travels behind a camera and sometimes wishes he was Michael Palin.

For a lot of Indians their gods are more of *sakha*s (friends) than authority figures, and this is how this woman returns home contently after offering her prayers at a temple in Maheshwar, Madhya Pradesh.

Pulse and Impulse: Rhythmic Journeys Through the Dances of India

Anita Ratnam

In the small alleyways of large cities and smaller towns, you will hear the sound of wood beating on wood. The faint sound of a staccato voice saying *tai ya tai, tai ya tai* may waft your way if you are driving through or stopping by a jasmine flower seller. Follow these sounds to their source and you will inevitably find a room filled with eager young girls, fresh from their school day, attempting a deep knee bend and striking their feet in consonance with the strident 'clackety clack' of the wooden stick.

This is a typical classical dance class in southern India. No matter what form of dance is being taught, young girls (and, rarely, some boys) begin or end their day learning basic classical dance alphabets or *etudes* from age six. From southern Tamil Nadu, through the meandering beaches of Kerala and the colourful villages of Karnataka and Andhra Pradesh, to the hills of Manipur way up in North-Eastern India and the alleyways of Lucknow in the state of Uttar Pradesh, dance and music is the warp and weft of this magnificent country. Classical, folk, tribal, martial and ritual dance styles define India's tryst with music and movement. Whether inside a darkened auditorium or under the open skies, dance and music was, and continues to pay homage to Nature and the supreme spirit.

India's is the only culture that has a dancing god as an icon. Shiva Nataraja with his wild hair, left leg crushing a small dwarf and right leg raised across the body into space, symbolises the harmony of the universe for philosophers and is a prime example of faultless symmetry for

Shiva, the supreme dancer. This iconic image conceives of the moment of creation as Shiva dances, uplifting the universe with the left upraised leg while trampling on ignorance.

sculptors and physicists. Of His four arms, two hold a drum and a flame to indicate rhythm and the impermanence of life respectively; the other two are held — palms facing forward and dropped down respectively — to bless and protect those who seek. This is possibly the most famous and recognisable image in museums, tourist shops and mantelpieces in homes. Shiva Nataraja, framed by a halo of fire, which says that all life begins and ends in a cyclical journey, *from* me *to* me.

It is not just our God who dances, but our heavenly nymphs too! Temple frescoes and myths abound with tales of dancing damsels who are so bewitching and lovely that even the stern sages — who swear abstinence from every passion succumb to their charms. A well-known legend is of sage Vishwamitra who was enamoured by the heavenly angel Menaka; their daughter Shakuntala married Prince Dushyanta and to them was born a son, named Prince Bharat, after whom India is named: Bharat.

One of the popular philosophical ideas that permeate many aspects of Indian culture is that of the *Ardha-Nariswara*, half man-half woman. It is not a mere point of view but represented in iconography via the sculpture of Shiva and his wife Parvati joined together in a single unit — the right side male and the left female. On the basis of this imagery and idea, there are two approaches to the dance tradition — *tandava* or the vigorous and energetic and *lasya* or the delicate and graceful. Shiva and Parvati, in turn, represent the ideals of virility and grace, as the original dancers from whom mortals learned this splendid art.

All of India's classical dance traditions reflect these polarities. Bharatanatyam contains an equal measure of both aspects. Its geometrical and rhythm-intensive repertoire attracts students from both genders. Performed only by women and originally called *sadir*, this popular dance style was restricted to the community of artistes called *isai vellalars*. The renaming of *sadir* to its present moniker Bharatanatyam and its

Odissi dance guru Kelucharan Mohapatra during one of his graceful performances.

subsequent impact on the modern history of Indian dance is a fascinating story.

In the early part of the twentieth century, stern Victorian values swept through India and many British as well as, English educated Indians were intent on 'cleaning up' the arts. Dancing women were referred to as 'nautch girls', an aberration from the Indian word *naach* or dance. Nautch was considered vulgar and nautch girls were frowned upon. Deprived of patronage from nobility and the wealthy connoisseurs of music and dance, musicians and dancers found it extremely difficult to continue the sacred art and their families were reduced to penury in the late nineteenth and early twentieth centuries. Some dancers were forced to subsist through sexual favours. This state of affairs was frowned upon by the colonials and a raging debate began in the English speaking societies of South India in favour of abolishing the nautch altogether. It was around the early 1930s that a lawyer, E. Krishna Iyer, who had learned *sadir* from one of the traditional teachers, led a debate at the Madras Music Academy with his famous line, "Don't throw out the baby with the bathwater." Iyer donned a traditional woman's dance costume and performed *sadir* to a packed auditorium of the city's elite to establish the beauty and richness of the classical art.

That watershed moment became a turning point that gathered momentum alongside India's march towards self-rule. Indians wanted to reclaim their lives and heritage on their own terms and dance became the centre of the cultural revival. Freedom fighters urged women from all sections of society to learn *sadir*. It was around the early 1940s that the dance form was renamed with a Sanskrit title — Bharatanatyam — the dance of India. Renaissance women from prominent Brahmin families like Rukmini Devi Arundale, a member of the Theosophical Society, began learning Bharatanatyam from a traditional teacher and launched her famous dance academy Kalakshetra in 1948.

Three decades earlier, Nobel laureate Rabindranath Tagore had begun welcoming artistes and thinkers to his new vision of an integrated and enlightened India. His West Bengal retreat called Shantiniketan, an idyllic locale, drew dancers, musicians, painters and thinkers and it became a crucible for the new arts of India. Bengal's distinctive style of soulful music called Rabindra Sangeet was born from these years of intense experimentation and creativity and the state also threw up an extraordinary dancer called Uday Shankar, who attained world renown with his pan-Indian style of performance drawn from many Indian classical dance traditions.

Uday Shankar's success in Europe and Rukmini Devi's renaissance thinking in Madras (now called Chennai), encouraged many women to learn classical dance. Through 1950s the Indian government established culture academies to promote and encourage the dance arts that were dwindling or dying out under colonial rule. This slow revival turned into a flood. By the late 1960s and early 1970s, classical dance became a prerequisite to a complete education, much like a finishing school. Girls were sent to dance and music classes after regular school hours. Dance debuts called *arangetram*s became popular. Rukmini Devi, encouraged by eclectic individuals of the Theosophical movement, challenged many male dominated ideas within the world of Indian classical dance. She encouraged women to learn how to conduct a dance performance. It was she who initiated the seating positions for dance accompanists to the right of the dancer on stage instead of entering the performance following the artiste as in a procession. She herself performed at the age of thirty-three, just to remind the new generation of free Indians that repossessing their art was an invaluable asset.

It is in this climate, bristling with the excitement of a new horizon, that several more dance styles of India grew and flourished. Odissi, Kuchipudi, Mohiniyattam, Kathakali and Kathak that were languishing in various parts of India quickly asserted their presence. States like West Bengal and Gujarat — which did not have indigenous classical dance forms — developed their folk dance traditions and encouraged creative experimentations in the arts.

Today, India has seven recognised styles of classical dance that are taught in varying degrees of popularity and demand.

Kathak dancer, Birju Maharaj, in a moment of ecstasy while executing a quick dance sequence.

After Bharatanatyam led the way in a newly independent India, it was Kathak, which rose to great popularity and acclaim among students in North India. This dance form with its swirling skirts and electric footwork is drawn from the opulent and hedonistic world of the Mughal courts. Kathak stems from the word *katha* or story. This is the only Indian classical dance style that does not have the bent-knee stance. From the predominant motif of entertainment, Kathak absorbed the stories of Indian myths and legends into its core repertoire. The stories of Lord Krishna, who was a mischievous divine child, dominate the Kathak repertoire, the highlight being the love songs and trysts between Krishna and the married older woman Radha.

All Indian dances draw their main narrative structures from the stories of Indian myths and legends. Besides the romantic adventures of Krishna, a perennial favourite is the *Ramayana*, the story of Prince Rama, his beautiful wife Sita and their adventurous lives through the forests of India. So also is the *Mahabharata* — the epic struggle of two families who battle through bloodshed and treachery for power. These two epics continue to inspire dancers from age seven to seventy with the variety of the human condition found in their pages. Since the oral tradition of storytelling and individual interpretation of legends is an inherent cultural motif, so too dancers explore each myth and story through the prism of their personal creative lens. This device in dance texts is called *sanchari* or exploration. It is this freedom that makes one performer unique from the other and the same material assumes various avatars in the hands of a truly imaginative artiste. In fact, written notation and copious notes is not the spine of music and dance training in India. Amidst strict tenets of

A group Kuchipudi choreography (left to right) — Radha, Yamini, Bhavana and Kaushalya Reddy with Raja Reddy seated in the centre.

formalism, it is the right of each teacher and student to explore and imagine, just like Western jazz practitioners hate to be constricted by codes and notation.

The structure of dance training and performance is phased out over five to seven years in which students learn the dance alphabet, *hasta-mudra*s or the hand gestures, the positions and movements of the feet, head, eyes, neck, limbs and torso. Each of the seven classical dance styles of India has differing emphasis on varying kinetic arcs. Some like Mohiniyattam, use the full body sway akin to the gentle sands and lazy waves of coastal Kerala; Manipuri takes the solitary mountains of Manipur's landscape and instills soft bobbing movements contained within gossamer veils and wired bulb like skirts or striped sarongs; Kuchipudi bounces with the energy of the warm countryside of Andhra Pradesh where red chillies and volatile tempers dominate. Sattriya, the most recent member of the classical dance roster, emphasises the devotional and graceful imagery of the gentle Assamese people.

Classical dance in India was once a sacred vocation. Women were dedicated to temples and served their local deity and the king with performances on festival days and birthdays of the royal family. These women, called *devadasi*s (servants of God) were highly respected, educated and independent. They owned property given to them by a patron or the king, earned money through teaching music and philosophy to the children of noblemen and were free to donate or bequeath their wealth to their daughters. Throughout India, dancing women in temples were admired and applauded. It is no wonder then that Victorian England looked upon these independent women with both fascination and horror.

In Orissa, young boys were part of a tradition of dressing up as women and performing acrobatic dances. They were called *gotipua*s and they travelled as a troupe to various towns to great acclaim. Today, these *gotipua*s still continue their unique tradition to remind us that Orissa has a rich tradition of men and women who perform dances suffused with devotion.

In fact, it is this hidden river of divinity that illuminates the dance traditions of India. Just as you would never see the name of the great sculptor who carved the giant frieze near shores of Mamallapuram in South India or the men who carved the breathtaking Sun Temple of Konarak in eastern India, so too the classical dancer is meant to dissolve the ego and become the vehicle for divine inspiration before each performance. *Natya* or dance is considered to be the fifth Veda, to educate and inspire those who cannot read or comprehend the esoteric meanings contained in the four great Sanskrit texts of India — *Rig*, *Yajur*, *Sama* and *Atharva Veda*s. It is *Natya* or dance/ theatre that is the form meant to carry the values of Indian civilisation and thought to the common man. Such is the importance and space given to the practice and performance of classical dance in Indian heritage.

Classical dance styles of India are as varied as the country itself. In a land that speaks so many languages, where the scripts and alphabets are so dissimilar and people from Assam and Manipur look more like their neighbours in Myanmar and where Kashmiris resemble the blue-eyed light skinned people of Afghanistan or Iran, this variety can be intimidating. Added to the plethora of sounds and rhythms are the different languages of Indian music that are the bedrock of classical dances. Bharatanatyam relies on Telugu and Tamil lyrics, Kuchipudi on Telugu, Kathak on Hindi and Urdu and Mohiniyattam on Malayalam and Sanskrit.

In fact, it is the classical language of Sanskrit that knits Indian dance styles together. Across the country, dancers from all the classical styles — Kathak, Manipuri, Sattriya, Odissi, Mohiniyattam, Kuchipudi and Bharatanatyam can perform differently to the same song in Sanskrit. An ode to Krishna, a verse from the *Rig Veda*, a homage to the dancing Shiva Nataraja or the beauteous Goddess Parvati can be the common strand to ignite the imagination of Indian dancers who cannot communicate to each other except through the language of *hasta-mudra*s and movements. Ironically, most Indians

today do not understand the language of the classical dance repertoire since modern spoken dialects are quite different from the classical origins of these languages. It is the universally recognised images of the dancing girl, bedecked with jewellery and flowers with ankle bells that have promoted the idea of Indian culture on posters and tourism offices overseas. When the Indian government under Prime Minster Indira Gandhi launched its international goodwill events in the early 1980s, classical dance was at the forefront. Famous artistes were sent as cultural ambassadors to all corners of the world and classical dance ensembles continue to represent India during important diplomatic and political missions.

The dances of India feature in the Indian sculpture, literature, painting, music and philosophy. Ancient temples are filled with dancing images in magnificent poses. The South Indian temples of Chidambaram and Sarangapani contain the 108 dance postures or *karana*s which are attempted by several students. To achieve a level of proficiency in classical dance is a lifelong pursuit, the dance-art being a 'calling' and not a mere skill.

Indian dance is often referred to as *visual music* and performances begin with a devotional song for good luck even before the dancer has entered the stage. With two distinct systems of classical music prevalent in India — North and South — the diversity and variety offered through these two disciplines can be seen clearly through the various classical dance forms of the country. The *Sama Veda* is considered to be the source of Indian music and the melodic structure of each song is meant to evoke specific moods when played or sung during each performance.

Both forms of music have the seven basic notes *Sa, Re, Ga, Ma, Pa, Dha, Ni* with five interspersed half notes, resulting in a twelve note scale. Unlike the twelve note scale in Western music, the base frequency of the scale is not fixed, and the inter-tonal gaps (temper) may also vary. Essentially, the roots of both forms of music are the same. North Indian music developed with the influence of Greek, Persian and Mughal cultures, while in the South, Carnatic music evolved independently.

Each performance in both the styles is set to a raga characterised in part by specific *arohana* or ascent and *avarohana* or descent sequences, which may not be identical. Each raga has a natural *ambit* or register and *meend* or glissando. Within all these rules, performances are marked with considerable improvisation. In Hindustani music the major vocal forms are the *Dhrupad, Khayal* and *Thumri*. Other forms include *Dhamar, Tarana, Trivat, Bhiti, Kajari, Tappa, Tap-Khayal, Ashtapadi*s, *Dadra, Ghazal* and *Bhajan*.

Carnatic music from the South tends to be more rigorous and rule-ridden, and abounds in the use of fixed compositions similar to Western classical music. Carnatic raga elaborations are generally much faster in tempo and shorter than their equivalents in Hindustani music. The opening piece is called a *varnam* and is a warm up for the musicians. A devotional hymn seeking the blessing of the Goddess Saraswati (for knowledge) or God Ganapati (to remove obstacles) follows. Then is a series of interchanges between ragas (unmetered melody) and *tala*s or rhythm. This is intermixed with other hymns called *kriti*s.

Both styles use a *tanpura* or a drone as a base note. They use definite scales to define a raga (a melodic pattern also spelled *raag*), but the Carnatic style employs *shruti*s or semitones to create a raga and thus has many more ragas than the North or Hindustani music style. While both styles sound very different, there are some common ragas with the same scale but are named differently. For instance, Hindolam raga in Carnatic is called Malkauns in the North, whereas Shankarabharanam and Bilawal raga are similar.

The word raga is derived from the Hindi word *rang* or colour and so each raga is expected to 'colour' the mind, bring delight, move the listeners and stimulate an emotional response. There are morning ragas like Ahir Bhairav, ragas for the afternoon like Madhyamavati and evening ragas like Kalavati. Listen to Shubapantuvarali and you may feel the mourning course through you like tears.

Tala is a vital component in Indian music and dance. The rhythm structures in dance can be mind numbing combinations

(*Pages 21 – 22*) Indian classical dancers practice their moves in the green room before they move on to the stage at Mandi House, New Delhi.

Pungcholam (dance) with wild yet controlled leaps and jumps while playing on the drum.

and teeth grinding sounds that pour out of the mouths of percussionists. Based largely on the five basic beat structures of three, four, five, seven and nine beat cycles, Indian dance and music rhythms can be exhilarating and intimidating at once. Accompanying the dancer is a group of musicians who are normally seated to her left on the stage. The conductor who wields, not the baton but a pair of small cymbals, leads the orchestra. He or she utters the pnemonic syllables or *chollu* to resonate with the rhythms played on the drums. Next to the conductor is seated a singer, a drummer, a violinist, flautist, a sitar player (for Kathak and Odissi) and a *veena* artiste (for Bharatanatyam and Kuchipudi). The variety of drums used for classical dance is a fascinating study in itself. There are so many various drum sounds in India created on so many surfaces that a separate study is often needed to understand the complexity of each instrument. Srident and aggressive are the *chenda* and *maddalam* of Kerala; the *mridangam*, *ghatam* and *ganjira* of Tamil Nadu and Andhra. Contrasting this apparent confidence is the gentle *edakkai* like the rolling waves for the white and gold maidens who perform Mohiniyattam. Sounds of the tabla, *dhol* and *pakhawaj* ripple across the stage for Odissi and Kathak dancers while *pung cholom* is the drum for the whirling dancer/drummers of Manipur.

While Indian classical dance traditions span three major areas — *nritta* or rhythm, *nritya* or expression and *abhinaya* or dramatic narrative, it is in the area of facial expressions that India stands unique. Nowhere else in the world is the human face explored and the range of human feelings and mental state expressed like in Indian dance. West of India, the face is not used in performance and towards the east, the face is covered with a mask. *Abhinaya* or facial expression is a fascinating Indian art that demands attention and applause for its depth, richness and emotive power. A master performer of seventy years can stay in one place and convey an entire story through her eyes, gestures and expression. Indian dance relies on one basic rule:

> Where the hand goes, the eye follows,
> Where the eye goes the mind joins,
> Where all three are in unison, the moment comes alive as *rasa*.

Rasa is also a uniquely Indian concept where the shared experience of the performer and viewer make up the collective experience. A *rasika* is the one who has empathy with the mood and the movements — both of the dance and the music that is being performed. A dancer comes alive in the presence of sensitive *rasika*s or an enlightened audience. This shared alchemy between the performer and her people is a vital prerequisite for a good performance. *Rasa* or flavour is the vital sap for an enjoyable evening.

As dance moved out of temples onto world stages and cultural tourism gained popularity in the country, folk and ritual dance forms of India began to attract attention. Temple festivals that adore the local deity or celebrate a festival of lights like Kartikai Deepam in South India are accompanied with temple instruments like the *nagaswaram* or horn instrument, *tavil* or drum and *irattai chinnam* or double reed trumpet. Traditional riffs called the *mallari* are played as the orchestra slowly marches in front of the deity that is carried on a palanquin or pulled on a giant chariot through the streets of the town or village. These festivals have a family of musicians attached to each temple, a tradition that is still followed in many sacred shrines throughout India. The local community of women may dance in front of the deity as it moves along the streets and flowers and chants accompany the celebrations as they travel. In mid-October, the festival of Navaratri, the nine days of the battle of the good and evil coincides with Ram Lila. The open fields in North India are decorated with giant effigies of King Ravana. At the end of the music and revelry, the enormous figure of the demon is burnt as a mark of his death and triumph of the valiant Rama.

In South India, ritual theatres like Yakshagana, Therukoothu, Theyyam and Koodiyattam are still practiced by male performers who don the roles of women and the stories of the *Mahabharata* and *Ramayana* are played out over several nights in village squares. Many performers are farmers during the day and take great pride in fulfilling their duty as actors when festival time approaches. Kerala's Theyyam is a terrific and terrifying trance dance to the Mother Goddess, and Koodiyattam contains the largest lexicon of hand

A Bharatanatyam dancer performs at the famous Tanjore Temple, Tamil Nadu at a dance fest.

gestures in classical dance art. Words, even verbs and adverbs, that are articulated in Koodiyattam have been recognised by UNESCO as a world heritage art.

Perhaps the most colourful of dance-theatre forms is Kathakali of Kerala. Again, this intricate and complex performance art was taught, learned and performed solely by men until the hegemony was challenged in the last twenty years. The elaborate makeup, costumes and headdress that take up to four hours to be put on; the specific colours — green, blue, yellow, red and black— representing the hero, villain and comic characters are a time-honoured tradition. Similar to the Greek theatre tradition of larger than life characters who occupy the middle level between the human and the divine, Kathakali actors employ the theatrical mode of 'catharsis' with their extreme theatricality and acting. These dramas are also stretched out over many nights, with the entire epic tales of Prince Rama or the great war between families in the *Mahabharata*, taking upto ten nights to perform. Watching in rapt attention would be the local populace, most of them familiar with the characters and the nuances of each gesture.

Distinctions between folk and classical forms are clear with each system either conforming to the larger Indian idea of *desi*, local and popular or *margi*, ancient and refined. These demarcations mean less today as many borders blur but folk dances in India are more varied and, at times, more exciting to watch than the classical dances. Created from amidst the communities, folk dances are a cyclical expression of the agricultural seasons — harvest, planting, monsoon — each time has songs, dances and celebrations. Men and women have their own dances, although this is the time when courting and flirting occur with matchmaking efforts at their most vigorous. Folk dances are also highly skilled forms and not for the common person to jump into. Costumes, music, lyrics and movements are learned by the respective peoples from a young age. Dancing during specific festivals is believed to bring good luck and encourage Nature to look kindly upon the planted crops. Some of the more popular folk dance forms of India are Ghumar, Bhangra, Kummi, KaiKottukali, Raas, Garba, Riang, Lai Haroba, Tera

Tali, Kacchi Ghodi and Kaliyattam. Feathered headgear, dummy horses, painted bodies, puppets, beaded clothing, clanging cymbals, clashing sticks — these dances are part trance, part celebration, different to the eye but synergised with Nature and the invisible Divine.

The twentieth century is called the time of greatest migration of the human race. It is also the time from the mid-sixties that Indian dance burst its geographical borders to take root 'in further soil'. From Alaska to Cape Town, Sydney to Moscow, classical dance schools sprung up all over the world, carried across the seas by immigrant Indians who married and sought their fortunes in foreign lands. In basements and newly built temples, classical dance teaching attracted several students, many from the immigrant population. Since Indian classical dance represents the various strands of Indian culture, parents were willing to drive several hours each way to give their children a 'taste of India' through dance classes. Today, at least 5,000 dance schools exist outside India teaching both Indian immigrants and the local citizen the finer points of Indian classical dance. From a solo dance tradition, group choreography has now become the norm to fill the large proscenium halls built across India. In the UK, USA and Canada, several generations of immigrants have absorbed this dance training into their own form now referred to as South Asian Dance. Bharatanatyam and Kathak are now familiar words in the UK alongside ballet and flamenco and are not attached to the 'idea' of India or Indian dance. Taking the rigorous classical training as a springboard, many choreographers have experimented with the formalism of the dance styles and created many exciting contemporary choreographies. Interaction with other musical genres like Western classical have also yielded interesting results with audiences, patrons and state funding ventures. The strong rhythmic structures of Indian classical dance and its inherent emotional content lend themselves successfully to cross cultural and mixed media adventures. The growing self-confidence of the Indian immigrant overseas has led to several articulate advocates and academic discussions on Indian dance in many international fora.

Sattriya dancers from Assam perform at a dance fest.

Look at the dances of India as a mirror of the exuberance of life itself. When you see the colourful powders in the marketplace, the smell of jasmine hanging outside shops, the crackle of freshly fried snacks and the soft jingle of ankle bells on women's feet; the rhythm of their swaying bodies and the pulse of their natural smiles — all these are mirrored in the dances of India. The formalism of the classical styles; the nature bound cycles of folk dances and the religious fervour of ritual theatre are but expressions of the millennia of life and experience that is the Indian civilisation. Do not agonise over technical terms like raga and *tala*. Don't trip up on words like *abhinaya* and *rasa*. Do not let your eyes glaze over with ideas like 'divinity' and 'sacred'. India is about joy and Indian dance reflects the paradigm of exuberance and silence. Like the circular red bindi dot that decorates women's foreheads, the centre of Indian dance is a fixed matrix — *bindu* — of harmony and beauty. The art that springs from that still centre is from the body and mind's core.

Each of the formal concepts I have shared with you is but a segue to help you enter into this fascinating world. All these ideas are like precious gemstones embedded into the gleaming fabric that is Indian dance. Surrender to the passion and the incredible artistry of a time honoured tradition. So listen to the simple sounds of wood on

wood emerging from a nearby lane and remember that hidden inside these modest classrooms could be a future master dancer carrying the incredible tradition of movement and gesture that is Indian dance, the pulse and impulse of India's life.

Anita Ratnam is a celebrated dancer who has traversed the different worlds of stage, television and the Internet through her performances, writings and public lectures. She is an important global voice on India's classical and contemporary dance traditions and continues her investigation into feminism, ritual and modernity.

(*facing page*) Contemporary Indian music has risen to wide appeal and has encouraged the Indian youth to learn and to combine traditional Indian sounds with the foreign.

A Kuchipudi dancer performs with her feet adorned with *ghungroo* (small metallic bells strung together) and *alta* (red colour paste applied at the sides of the feet).

(*facing page*) Ustad Bismillah Khan, renowned master of an Indian wind instrument called the *shehnai*.

Legendary Carnatic singer M.S.Subbulakshmi.

Art from India

Anjum Katyal

I remember how, in the nineties, it seemed that every second housewife with time on her hands was opening a 'boutique' — suddenly there was an explosion of demand for 'designer' ethnic wear. Today, one sees the same thing with art galleries. Almost anyone with room to spare is opening a gallery, so much so that the gallery seems to have become as ubiquitous as the local *modi* (corner grocery) store. Every neighbourhood has one. And if one considers the number of sleek, glossy art exhibition invitation cards courier-delivered to the door, and even sleeker, glossier catalogues, replete with expensive full-colour reproductions of art works; it seems fair to say that the business of art in India is flourishing.

To someone who has been involved with the contemporary art scene in India since the mid-eighties, the recent explosion of general interest, media coverage, exhibitions, galleries, dealers and, of course, prices is a cause of amazement. Today's top Indian artists are household names, at least amongst the elite and the aspiring elite. A work of art on your wall is a status symbol, an indication of taste and discrimination. Prices have escalated to such a degree that even students fresh out of art school can command a good rate. Young, upwardly mobile, just marrieds are picking up paintings for new homes. Dealers, businessmen and art trusts are making shrewd investments in art. Indian artists are exhibiting widely abroad. Prestigious international auction houses like Sotheby's and Christie's are scheduling regular auctions of Indian art, which is also being widely viewed, bought and sold on the Internet. To some, all this is a reflection of a growing economy and the availability of disposable income. To others, it is a just and overdue recognition of the excellence of Indian artists. Whatever the reason, it is fair to say that Indian art or should we say art from India, since we shall shortly see that there is no single entity known as 'Indian' art, has come of age. The Indian artist is accomplished, confident, and on par with his peers anywhere in the world.

A *nayak* (hero) plucking a thorn from the foot of the *nayika* (heroine). The theme, explored extensively by Indian artists and even Indian cinema, corresponds with the concept of love in India.

The first thing that strikes us about the Indian art scene is its infinite variety. Walk into any gallery or browse the Internet, and you will see such a range of styles and subject matter that it is impossible to categorise this art. From abstraction to symbolic or tantric motifs; from intricately detailed figurative work to delicate watercolour washes; from traditional subject matter — village scenes, rickshaws, Varanasi — to the kitsch of popular culture; from vivid colours to vegetable and natural dyes to the subtlest of palettes; from canvases meant to be hung on a wall to multimedia constructions and installations meant to be experienced or interacted with, all are equally part of today's art scene. Whatever your own personal taste in art, you are bound to find a celebrated artist or talented beginner to patronise. In order to appreciate how all this rich diversity came about, we need to retrace our steps to understand how we reached where we are today. Anyone who has read Indian history in school knows that the Indian art heritage stretches way back into antiquity. From ancient times to the twenty-first century, there is a wealth of art tradition for contemporary Indian artists to draw upon.

The very first artefacts dug up at archaeological sites like Mohenjodaro display developed aesthetic and established conventions. Ancient texts outline theories of colour and aesthetics, and anecdotal accounts suggest that it was common for households to have painted doorways, facades and rooms. Cave paintings from Ajanta, Bagh and Sittanvasal, temple painting, temple and rock carvings remain with us as a reference that shows up in contemporary art in various ways. The Chola art of South India and the frescoes of Ajanta and Ellora in particular were to have a great influence on Indian artists centuries later.

The medieval period had its Rajput, Mughal and Pahari paintings, miniatures and illuminated manuscripts — free of the 'vanishing point perspective' that came to dominate Western art after the Renaissance, and full of storytelling. There was also the abstract, geometric, stylised decorative art and calligraphy favoured by Islam; and of course the grace and space of medieval architecture — forts, monuments, tombs, palaces, caravanserais and gateways.

And down the centuries there has always been the vibrant, living folk art — decorative, symbolic and narrative — which we can still see on village walls and scroll paintings. Warli painting, with its delicate stick figures set in space, telling of the activities of daily life; the *pat* paintings of eastern India in which successive frames tell a story in full colour and vibrant figuration; the bright and colourful

Madhubani of Bihar which combines figures with ornamental motifs; Mysore and Tanjore paintings from South India, which decorate the composition with gold, enamel, fabric, beads and glass, are some of the local regional art forms which continue to inspire today's artists. Another set of inputs that has influenced modern Indian artists consists of the aesthetics of tantric philosophy, with its symbolic use of form and colour.

With the advent of the Europeans came Western approaches to art. The most significant of these were: the 'single point of view', leading to a fixed perspective; Western ideas of composition; the individuality of an artist's expression; the play of light and shadow, or chiaroscuro; and naturalism (the creation of volume or a three-dimensional effect, leading to 'realistic' representational art). The introduction of the painted canvas or sculpture as an object to be hung on a wall or displayed in a room was also an innovation from the West. Soon local artists were introducing these ideas into their work. With new technology, new media such as prints and woodcuts also came in, and by the nineteenth century, between the princely state capitals and the British cities, there was a wide variety of hybrid art forms and styles available to the common man, from 'Company painting' to theatre backdrops, to the Battala and Kalighat prints of Calcutta (now Kolkata). The stagey 'scenes' of Raja Ravi Varma and others like Hemen Mazumdar from Bengal, in which graceful damsels in exotic drapery pose against romantic backgrounds, the titles endowing them with a historical or mythological lineage, came to be known as 'calendar' art, a new popular art very much along the lines of what was being produced in Europe at the time. Photography was another new media that began to take its place in the gallery of art forms.

Promoting Western academic training, with its emphasis on draftsmanship, life study, nature study, composition, perspective and natural dimensions, were the government colleges of art, in Calcutta, Madras (now Chennai) and the Sir J.J. School of Art in Bombay (now Mumbai). Set up in the late nineteenth and early twentieth century, these institutions have long lists of illustrious alumni, including some of today's biggest names.

(*facing page*) Madhubani painting on paper illustrating much loved Indian god Rama, with wife Sita and brother Lakshman being ferried across River Ganga.

Tanjore painting of the deity Krishna, at the Nathwara Temple, holding aloft the Govardhana Giri.

As nationalism began to take hold, there was a gathering resistance to British cultural imperialism, including Western aesthetics and ways of approaching art. Calcutta was the centre of what came to be known as the Bengal School, led by Abanindranath Tagore, which was inspired by older, 'traditional' Indian styles such as the medieval miniature and the art of Ajanta-Ellora, as well as Japanese aesthetics. Delicacy, subtlety, restraint, romanticism, and historical, mythological or symbolic subject matter were characteristic of their output, with the most widely used medium being a soft watercolour wash. The aesthetics of the Bengal School, closely allied with a growing pride in indigenous culture and India's glorious art inheritance, and with the nationalist movement on the whole, was to have a major influence on art practice in the country, so much so that in the forties there was a strong reaction to it.

Standing apart was the towering figure of Rabindranath Tagore who brought in a modernism unseen till then. In the early twentieth century we also had Amrita Shergill who returned to India with her Parisian training and turned her eye on Indian subjects conveyed in an Indian palette. Jamini Roy, working in Bengal, took the local folk aesthetic of toys, dolls and *pat* painting and turned it into modern art.

In Calcutta, the Calcutta Group was formed in 1943 in reaction to both the dominant trends of Western academism and the Bengal School. It sparked off fresh thinking, inducting contemporary ideas from the international arena. The founding artists were Nirode Mazumdar, Prodosh Das Gupta, Rathin Moitra, Subho Tagore, Prankrishna Paul, Gopal Ghose and Paritosh Sen. The Indian College of Arts and Draftsmanship (earlier Indian Art School) was another venerable institution that produced leading figures like the late Bikash Bhattacharjee, whose surreal paintings turned him into one of the most sought-after painters of his time; the reclusive Ganesh Pyne whose mastery over tempera has made him one of the

country's best known names; and others like Sunil Das, and the late Shyamal Dutta Ray — together they formed the highly regarded Society of Contemporary Artists. Historically at the vanguard of cultural innovation and experimentation, Kolkata has produced a high percentage of nationally renowned artists, and though today the cutting edge of the art scene has moved away to other metros, the city is still home to the leading artists mentioned above, along with some younger ones too.

Shantiniketan, close to Calcutta, and the site of Rabindranath Tagore's great experiment in education, became an important centre of the arts in early twentieth century. Abanindranath Tagore, with whom the Bengal School is famously associated, worked here, and a circle of eminent artists — Benodebihari Mukherjee, Nandalal Bose, Ramkinkar Baij — taught and practiced in its peaceful atmosphere, conducive to creative excellence. Although following differing styles, their work, very broadly, was descriptive and interpretive, capturing and conveying a mood rather than telling a story. They turned to local and indigenous subjects and styles for inspiration. Continuing from where they left off, eminent artists like the late Somnath Hore, K. G. Subramanyan and Jogen Chowdhury, who based themselves in Shantiniketan, helped promulgate an atmosphere of artistic creativity that has ensured Shantiniketan's presence as an important art centre. Even today, young artists and teachers at the arts faculty are playing an active role in the contemporary art scene.

Baroda developed into another major art centre in the decades after Independence. The Faculty of Fine Arts, Maharaja Sayajirao University, became the centre of the Baroda School, known for its narrative driven work full of figures, storytelling and shifting perspectives. The artists told stories drawn from their own lives and those of the city that surrounded them, as well as the wider world of politics. They too rebelled against the British academic style of painting and the Bengal School, even as they turned to other indigenous craft and folk traditions of the country as sources of inspiration. Under the guidance of senior artist K. G. Subramanyan, a community of committed

art practitioners began to make waves throughout the country and abroad with their fresh and often controversial ideas. He himself set the tone with robust black humour and satirical eye, telling multiple stories in multiple frames. Bhupen Khakhar's introduction of homoeroticism and bazaar kitsch; Gulam Mohammad Sheikh's depiction of the horrors of the Baroda riots of the mid-eighties, and his invocation of Kabir as a voice of inter-religious amity; Nilima Sheikh's concern with poetry, history, politics and women's issues, are some of the more notable features of these artists' work. Baroda has contributed many younger artists who are doing interesting work today.

Mumbai has the Sir J.J. School of Art, established in the 1850s, with its long list of famous alumni, including K.H.Ara, S.H.Raza, F.N. Souza, Akbar Padamsee, Laxman Pai, K.K.Hebbar, V.S. Gaitonde and amongst the younger artists, Atul Dodiya, Jitesh Kallat, Bose Krishnamachari, Sudarshan Shetty and many more. Bombay also had, in the late forties, on the heels of the Calcutta Group, the Progressive Artists' Group. Motivated by a similar rejection of the aesthetics and 'nationalism' of the Bengal School and determined to introduce the experiments of European modernism, the Progressive Artists' Group included Souza, Raza, M. F. Hussain (arguably India's most famous, controversial, and highly priced artist), S. K. Bakre, Akbar Padamsee and Tyeb Mehta. Widely different in terms of individual style, they can said to be linked by a common interest in introducing an international language into their art practice, though some of them deliberately turned to Indian themes. By 1956 the group had disbanded, but former members continue to sound like a who's who of Indian art.

Delhi too was home to some of the country's best known art names, such as the late J. Swaminathan, who in the early sixties was one of the founders of Group 1890, against 'vulgar naturalism', the 'pastoral idealism' of the Bengal School, and the 'hybrid mannerism' of European modernism. In his painting he employed the symbolism of tribal art. Satish Gujral, deeply inspired by Mexico's exuberant and vigorous muralists, is one of Delhi's most senior artists. Manjit Bawa, who passed away recently, will be remembered for his pristine colours

The artist imparts detail to the idol in the right upon finishing the first coat of the one on the left at his workshop in Kolkata.

and still figures. Manu Parekh, Madhvi Parekh, Anjolie Ela Menon and Arpita Singh are other well known Delhi based artists. Manu Parekh's Benaras canvases and drawings of anthropomorphic forms still draw attention. Madhvi Parekh chooses to employ the simplicity, power and fullness of folk art in her paintings. Anjolie Ela Menon's gently melancholic female figures set against architectural forms and interiors in melodious colours have won her great popularity; while Arpita Singh's busy surfaces are filled with objects, bodies and stories.

Down south, there was the Cholamandal group, led by K. C. S. Panicker, who combined aspects of the mystic with text and graffiti in a shift away from the confines of perspective; while in Hyderabad the work of K. Laxma Goud and D. L. N. Reddy resurrected the human figure.

A workshop at Experimental Art Gallery in India Habitat Centre, New Delhi.

In the genre of sculpture, historically India has had a wide range of ancient and medieval styles to offer — free-standing and in relief, in metal, wood and stone — and in colonial times the Western Greco-Roman or naturalist style was added to this gallery of choices. Since working with traditional materials has always been expensive, there have been far fewer sculptors down the decades throughout the country than painters. Ramkinkar Baij of Shantiniketan is celebrated for his large free-standing figures and clusters of common men and women; in the seventies, eighties and nineties Meera Mukherjee studied the tribal Bastar lost wax process of metal sculpture and incorporated it in her pathbreaking modern pieces, while Somnath Hore's poignant bronze figures, speaking of loss and dispossession, remain amongst the most highly regarded works of Indian sculpture. Today, the outsize fibreglass heads of South Indian women by Ravinder Reddy, amongst other contemporary sculpture, signal a move towards newer materials, including found objects.

For the past decade, however, it is no longer possible to identify dominant 'schools' or clearly classify artists from different cities and locations. Nor does it seem relevant to talk of discrete genres like sculpture or painting in oil, tempera, or watercolour. Many strains, influences and trends have interwoven like multicoloured strands to produce the tapestry that is the Indian art scene today. India's glorious, ancient art heritage is one set of inputs; international influences ranging from Europe, the US, Islamic art, Japan, cinema, photography and popular culture (such as comic books, advertisements and poster art) are another set of inputs. The result is the broad spectrum of art being produced in India today. Which is why, although we have plenty of art from India, it is not so easy to define 'Indian art'.

Like their counterparts throughout the world, today's artists from India are employing a wide range of media in their work. Paint on canvas is now just a small part of the process. All sorts of materials — found and created, and technology, electronic inputs, sound, light, projection, digital media, are being used. From being an artefact to hang on the wall or admire on a pedestal, a work of art is now more often an experience, demanding participation and interaction. We enter an environment created by the artist, to which we respond not just with our eyes, but with our whole bodies — touching, hearing, and feeling. In terms of form and media, there is little to distinguish art from India from art produced anywhere in the world.

And yet being rooted, having a context, being grounded, are very important conditions of artistic creativity. All artists necessarily work within a social, cultural and economic framework. The images they access, the themes and subject matter of their work, reflect their particular reality. It is, therefore, only natural for the work of Indian artists to reflect an 'Indianness' somewhere, even if it is only a reference. This Indianness may be central (like Thota Vaikuntham's dark and curvaceous females after the South Indian Tanjore style of art, or Lalu Prasad Shaw's exquisite, frozen figures after the miniature style of art) or incidental (like Chittrovanu Mazumdar's modified digital images of the gradually disintegrating carcass of a calf rotting into the earth of Jharkhand, in the heart of rural India). Another example is the sculpture and installation of Subodh Gupta which revisits the everyday products and objects of rural life in his native Bihar, such as cooking utensils, milk buckets, and dried cowdung cakes. Somewhere this life experience marks the output of artists from India — so that if there is one feature common across all the differences, it is perhaps this.

M. F. Hussain (b.1915), famously India's highest priced artist, his tall, lean, upright figure with his full head of white hair and white beard, bare feet and long paintbrush for walking stick, are iconic. He has also drawn more than his fair share of controversies over the years. Born in Pandhapur, Maharashtra, Maqbool Fida Hussain learned the art of calligraphy from a young age; he also learned to write poetry, an art that has stayed with him since. In 1937 he went to Bombay, determined to become an artist. Years of struggle followed, during which he painted cinema hoardings to make two ends meet. In 1947 he won an award at the annual exhibition of the Bombay Art Society, and began to be noticed. He joined the prestigious and pioneering Progressive Artist's Group. By 1955 he was a well-known name and had been awarded the Padma Shri by the Indian government. He was a special invitee, along with

Pablo Picasso, at the Sao Paulo Biennial in 1971. Hussain was awarded the Padma Bhushan in 1973, the Padma Vibhushan in 1989 and was nominated to the Rajya Sabha in 1986. He has also made several films, some of which have won awards at international festivals. His strong sense of colour and graphic design, and his penchant for responding promptly to national issues, are his hallmarks.

Meera Mukherjee (1923 – 1998) is one of India's best known sculptors, unequalled in her innovative use of the traditional tribal lost wax process of bronze sculpture. Born in Kolkata, she studied at the Government Art College in Calcutta, followed by the Delhi Polytechnic, after which

A Warli painting in the house of a tribal settled in the Dahnu district of Maharashtra. The Warli paintings depict their way of life, their rituals and customs. Here the painting shows them celebrating harvesting of crop (paddy) in monsoon, with a man playing their local musical instrument *Tarpu* and women dancing around.

she received a scholarship to study in Munich in 1953, under Toni Stadler and Heinrich Kirchner. From 1957 she began her study and work with the tribal artisans of Bastar and the bell metal craftsmen of Central India. In the sixties she began to receive recognition for her work; and in 1968 the President conferred on her the Master Craftsman in metalwork award. Deeply influenced by folk *dhokra* metal sculpture, her work features ordinary men and women engaged in everyday tasks — stitching, winnowing, riding a crowded bus, fishing, weaving, labouring, singing, dancing, playing — with a delicacy and fluid energy that transcends the rigidity of the metal medium. Her towering Ashoka and baul musicians remain outstanding examples of public sculpture.

K. G. Subramanyan (b. 1924), born in a village in Kerala, he became actively involved in the freedom struggle as a young boy, even doing a stint in jail and finally finding himself banned from studying in government colleges during the British Raj. When his talent for art was noticed, he was encouraged to apply to Shantiniketan, which he did in 1944. This was a turning point in his development as an artist. Till 1948 he studied under pioneers of modern art and the Bengal School such as Nandalal Bose, Benodebehari Mukherjee and Ramkinkar Baij. In 1951, he joined the Faculty of Fine Arts in Maharaja Sayajirao University, Baroda, and became influential in developing what is known as the Baroda School. He has always encouraged a strong interest in the folk and craftsman traditions of the country. His tenure at Baroda was interrupted

by brief stints in London and New York. In 1980 he returned to his alma mater to teach at Kala Bhavan, contributing to a revival of Shantiniketan as a centre for the arts. He continued to live there after retirement, as Professor Emeritus, till he moved back to Baroda after his wife passed away in 2005. Mani-da, as he is widely and respectfully known, is one of the most highly regarded practising artists, theoreticians, teachers and writers in the world of Indian art today.

Arpita Singh (b. 1937) was born in West Bengal, though she now lives in New Delhi. She studied at the School of Art, Delhi Polytechnic, Delhi from 1954 – 59. Having spent some years working for the Indian Government's Cottage Industries restoration programme, which entailed close interaction with traditional artisans and craftsmen, folk aesthetics came to play a large role in her work. In the eighties she produced watercolours on paper showing the simple daily activities of Bengali women; in the nineties she shifted to canvas. Her portrayals of women's lives and concerns continue to be a major theme in her work. Along the lines of folk art, her surfaces tend to be filled with multiple figures and details. She has exhibited widely both within and outside the country.

Anjum Katyal is a professional editor with a strong focus on arts and culture publishing. She was Editor and then, Editorial Director, with a Kolkata based publishing house, and is now, Editor, Saregama-HMV. Since the eighties, she has been involved with organising art exhibitions, writing catalogue pieces, editing a theatre journal and undertaking several translations. She also writes poetry in English and sings the blues.

The inauguration of a painting exhibition at the Open Palm Court at the India Habitat Centre, New Delhi.

(*Pages 43 – 44*) Nawalgarh Shekhawati, Rajasthan: Indian art is warmly inclusive of all — from the elaborate Indian mythology to the rich Indian history. It does not stand isolated but converses with the daily life.

The Living Crafts of India: Unbroken Continuities

Ritu Sethi

In today's India across villages, hamlets, tribal swathes and urban fringes, in the most unlikely of places, ancient craft and weaving technologies are practiced and preserved, sometimes tenuously, often transmitted orally from father to son, mother to daughter, guru to *shishya*. The dexterity and skill of India's craftspersons, their use of indigenous and ecologically viable technology to imagine and create, to weave, smell, mould, sculpt, engrave, paint, build and imagine spans a cultural landscape that has for many millennia been shaped and bound together by its history, mythology and legend. They are ingeniously adapted to surrounding nature, attuned to abundance and scarcity, and connected with social and ritual demand.

The beginnings of India's craft traditions lie in the first known settled civilisation of the subcontinent in the cities of the Indus Valley. This formed the blueprint for a continuous 5,000 year journey, formulating ways of thinking and seeing with closely defined links with the elements, a direction for the arts and a social structure that remains rooted till today. Over the course of history, waves of rulers and ruling empires, migrating people and craftspersons, merchants who plied the inland and maritime trade routes, travellers and scholars, have provided an exchange point for material possessions, ideas, languages, customs and cultures. To the present day, this complex culture is influenced by

A child plays cricket near his house in Ahmedabad, not worried
about the ready earthen pots behind.

happenings and events in the globalised world, yet absorbs and makes them its own. For instance, from the scroll painter in West Bengal who painted the cataclysmic 9/11 event and sings movingly about it; the Rajasthani folk puppet vigorously being manipulated to a disco beat; the *sujani* embroiderers from Bihar sew messages of AIDS awareness; the Jhara tribals who cast a message to the Prime Minister in metal; the Madhubani artist who draws the coming of the railway to her part of the world, to the fine *chikan* embroidery of Lucknow destined for the haute couture fashion houses of Paris and New York. These and many more are shaping our vision for tomorrow.

It is estimated that at present there are over 23 million craftspersons in India — making this sector second only to agriculture in its scope of self-employment — with over 360 clusters spread across the country. A little over 76 per cent of these are located in India's rural hinterland. Clusters are individualised and differentiated by the craftspersons' inventive responses to habitation, environment and demand — for objects for the sacred, for the temporal and for the everyday. About 96 per cent of the craftspeople create by crafting within their own household space and by drawing on the services of kith and kin. Each of them provides a necessary skill — from spinning the *charkha* to dyeing the yarn, the making of a bobbin to the laying of the warp and weaving the loom.

The diversity and plurality of India's craft tradition extends to the creators of craft themselves. India has over 460 scheduled tribe communities distinguished by their language and dialects, by their dress, headgear, ornaments and tattoos and by their rich oral traditions, music, dance and culture. The communities have skilled storytellers and craftspersons proficient in metallurgy, carving, pottery, painting, basketry and other crafts. The itinerant artisan is as remarkable — be it the Lohar wrought iron makers of Bastar, the Banjara embroiderers of Andhra Pradesh, the lost wax metal casters of Jharkhand, Chattisgarh and Orissa or the Jadupatua scroll painters and bard healers of the Santhal tribe.

In a country where caste occupations are inherited, craftspersons are seen as descendants of Lord Vishwakarma, the architect of the gods to whom a large number of craftspersons trace their origin. Practicing either individually or in clusters, whole villages and pilgrimage towns are sometimes known equally for their craft practice. For instance, the bronze casters of Swamimalai; the potters of Molela; Pichwai painters of Nathdwara; the block printers of Bagh, Bagru, Balotra, Dhamadka, Sri Kalahasti, Machlipatnam, Kal Dera; Mithila painters of Madhubani; the leather footwear makers of Kolhapur; the painters of Raghurajpura and the hand paper makers of Sanganer. The migrant craftspersons in urban centres like the *zari* embroiderers of Delhi and Kolkata, add to the list.

Responding with inventiveness to the country's strongly contrasting geographic features of landscape, climate and topography, Indian craftspersons have developed a domestic technology adapted to the environment and to materials available and connected with demand. One can see this from the wool gathering and weaving of the pashmina shawls in the upper reaches of the Himalayas; the gathering of the *al* root to create the characteristic red; the weaving of wild *eri* and *muga* silk of Assam; the variety of creative responses to wild grass, fibre and vegetation that grows in abundance, and the sculpturing of *shola* pith in West Bengal; the toys and baskets of *sikki* grass in Bihar and Orissa, and the use of *kauna* reed to make mats in Imphal; the *kora* mats of Kerala and Tamil Nadu, the use of wicker in Kashmir; the mats of *sheetalpati* and *masland* in Assam and West Bengal, the use of *sarkhanda* in Haryana to make furniture and containers, and of the *pulla* grass footwear of Himachal; the ubiquitous use of cane and bamboo across the North-East and in other parts to build homes and bridges, flutes, *chiks*, baskets to beer mugs. The list is endless.

A close relationship with everyday life also underpins Indian handicrafts, as does its sensitivity to natural and seasonal rhythms. Common objects for daily needs are created by potters, weavers, metal smiths, jewellers and dyers. Combining indigenously developed technologies with locally available materials, local skills and local needs, the objects created are functional, utilitarian and practical. Unlike assembly line production, where products are made

(*Page 47*) A potter immersed in his art at Necklace Road, Hyderabad.
(*Page 48*) Terracotta pots at Uttam Nagar, New Delhi.

A craftsman working on a copper plate in New Delhi.

for distant markets and unknown users, these handicrafts — even the smallest and most insignificant ones — are personalised for the user, embellished and adorned with a vernacular idiom of form and visual expression. The range is as marvellous as the attention to details — from butter churners to vegetable slicers and other kitchen accessories; from icons for worship to locks and latches for safety; from writing instruments to *lota*s and spouted pots from women's beauty accessories and makeup containers to hookahs and chillums for the man of the house; from scales and measures for trade to children's toys, games and dolls.

Parallel to the development of humble everyday craft, grew ritual crafts based on belief systems of organised religion, ancient folk wisdom, and innumerable cults, religious sects and ways of thought. The classical craft tradition that flowered around temples built to glorify and worship gods departs from the folk and tribal traditions. Till date, these follow strict rules laid down in *Shilp Shastra*s, pertaining to iconography and iconometry, with shape, proportion, colour, stance, and use of material dictated in a manner appropriate to honouring the gods. These rules of measurement apply not only to religious and secular architecture but also to functional objects used for offerings for the celebrant, the priest and the community.

The ritual offerings of the folk traditions, with their spontaneity and fluidity of vision, made myths and legends come to life. Whether it is the daily making of auspicious symbols on the doorstep to ward off evil, or terracotta figures with symbolic attributes one can spot their immediacy and relevance. Local deities, the *gram devata*s, guardians of rural life, the larger than life terracotta horses offered to Lord Aiyannar, a village deity, are to be seen in villages across Tamil Nadu. Phad cloth panel paintings of Rajasthan depicting the epic adventures of Dev Narayan, a folk hero, the Bhoota cult figures of nature spirits carved in wood in Dakshin Karnataka and cast in bronze and bell metal in Udipi, the block printed and painted shrine cloth *mata ni pachedi* of Gujarat depicting the Mother Goddess are all part of daily lives and imaginings.

A visitor appreciates a statue of Lord Mahavir at India International Centre, New Delhi.

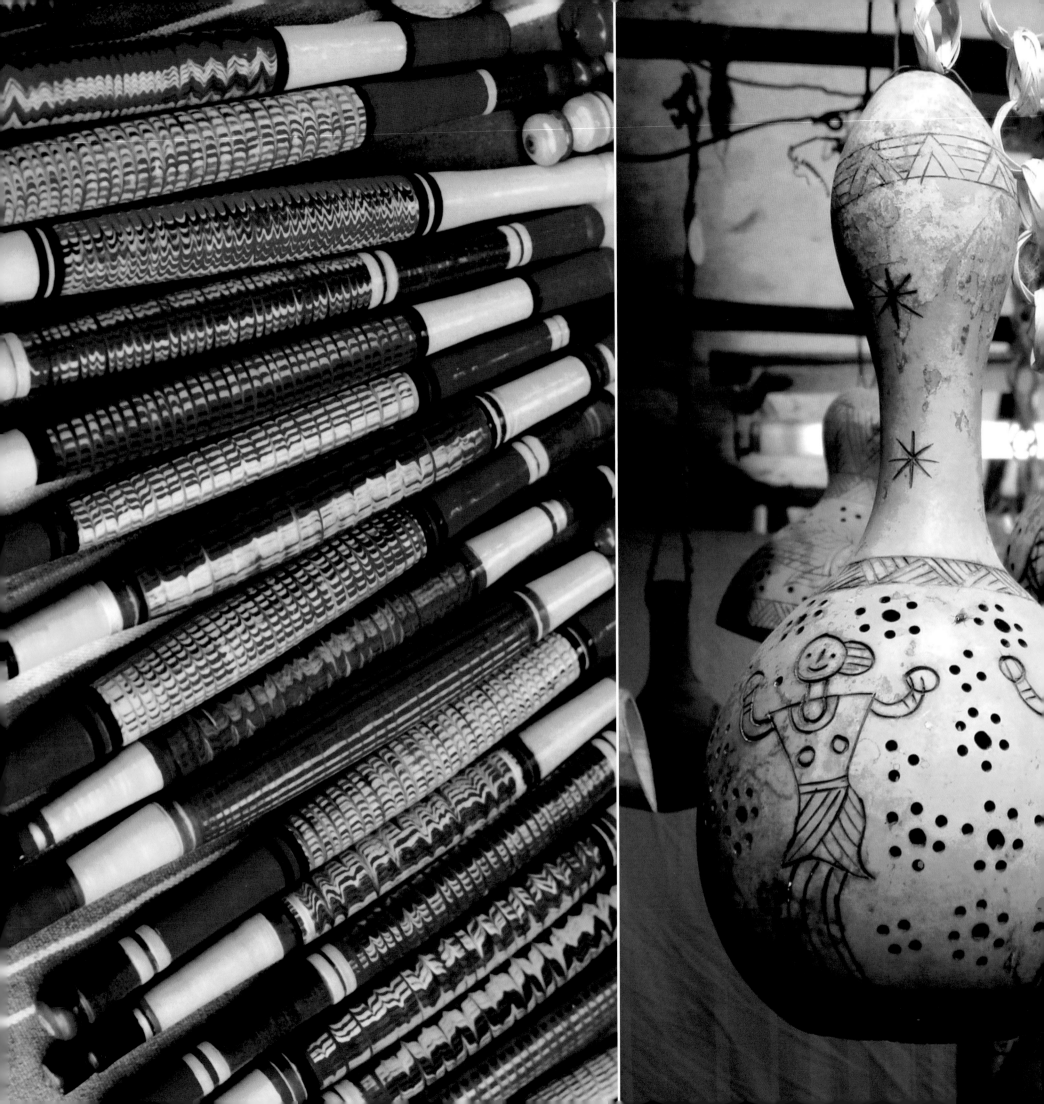

Bearing a stamp of achievement that is not only indigenous and ancient but also notably creative, is the ritual and everyday art of India's tribal communities — whether it is the tribal textiles in heavy cotton, dyed in madder and black obtained from waste iron worn by the Oraon, Muria, Maria, Dhurva and Gonds; or the abstract wall pictographs of the Warli tribe of Maharashtra.

Along the continuum of crafts were the efflorescence of

luxury and court crafts that were intimately bound to politics, trade and the pursuit of a privileged life. These included woven silks, jewellery, carpets, metal ware, muslins likened to woven air, dyed and printed textiles, embroideries, shawls — and endless array of objects both desired and envied.

The insatiable appetite for India's fabled artefacts, along with continuing traditions of craftsmanship, demonstrate the high level of skill that has survived in India till today. From the brocade weaving in Varanasi, to the metal casting in Swamimalai; from the *kundan* and enameled *minakari* jewellery of Jaipur to the *pachikari* semi-precious stone inlay of Agra; from the *thewa* gold leaf worked on the glass of Pratapgarh to the continuing tradition of kalamkari patterned textiles of Machlipatnam, once meant for the elite in Europe and Britain — objects that continue to be highly prized and regarded, these also remained gifts fit for kings, and today, for exchange between heads of state.

Equally bright and joyful are the festive crafts. All over India, festivals are celebrated and icons, lights, objects, ephemeral in nature are crafted — from the construction of the effigy of Ravana, the demon king built with paper, bamboo and filled with fire crackers to Uttarayana celebrated in Ahmedabad with the flying of paper kites with craftspersons travelling from all over to make patterned kites and cotton thread strengthened with crushed glass, from kite flying with a contemporary twist with kites in the colours of the Indian flag made especially for and flown on 15 August as a symbol of freedom on the Independence Day to the *sanjhi* floor decorations created with intricately cut paper stencils, filled in with colours, celebrating events in the life of Lord Krishna; from the elaborate clay Ganpathi in Maharashtra, worshipped and then ritually relinquished into the waters to the folk tradition of making of Goddess Sanjhi in Haryana and Rajasthan; from the cow dung votives and the floral arts made for celebrations, gifts, events and as presentations to the ritual floor mandalas and symbols on the floors and walls; from the Buddhist butter sculptures to the Muslim Tazziya — they are all painstaking and elaborately made.

(*Pages 53 – 54*) Wooden lac rolling pins, Sankheda, Gujarat (*left*), Lac bangles, Rajasthan (*centre*), Decorated dried gourds that have been converted into lamps, Dilli Haat, New Delhi (*right*).

Tilla Jutti (Embroidered footwear) of Haryana.

Festivities and *mela*s are memorable for their playful and inventive toys and dolls for children made of clay, tinsel, palm fronds, coconut fibre, papier mâché, wood and other material.

The tools used in crafting objects and weaving of textiles range from the most simple and basic to the technologically complex, using scientific and mathematical principles and employing an extraordinary knowledge of material combined with an inventive mind and the ability to think spatially and visually. Tools are often made to suit the hand and eye of the user, and personalised to age and physique — not available over the counter, in shops or markets. The makers of the tools are often the craftspersons themselves or craft 'engineers' working within the traditions of an oral and hereditary knowledge system that is closely unified in its understanding of material and process. The tools range from the inventive construction of a bent bicycle spoke, to burn geometric designs on to a tribal wind pipe; from the intricately carved wooden block used for textile patterning, to the loin loom of the North-East made to suit the woman's form and convenience as she weaves in her open courtyard; from the loom designed for the double ikat *patola* silk sari of Patan built so that two weavers can work simultaneously to the balanced potters' wheel; from the tribal crucible, moulds, lathe, files and chisels to cast the lost wax *dhokra* metal object to the bamboo pen used to paint the translucent goat skin of the leather puppets of Andhra Pradesh; from the iron drawing chisel used to engrave the intricate geometric and floral patterns on the black metal Bidriware to the ubiquitous *dao*, the curved, razor sharp knife of the North-East craftsperson used to split bamboo and perform the most delicate of tasks.

Honed with time, these methods and processes of creation can be simple or complex with multiple and sequential processes, but there always is unity between the maker and the material. Days or months go in the making and the identity of the maker is often recognisable, almost branded into a product. Similarly, the understanding of the chemical and physical properties of plant and fibre to be used as dyes, create textiles, plait ropes, weave mats, use as thatching, make into paper is unparalleled and unsurpassed.

A sari at Dilli Haat, New Delhi displaying Kantha work, a textile tradition native to West Bengal.

The time honoured situation of the craftsperson as designer blending aesthetics, technical skills and marketing has come under strain with craft products vying with machine made products. Crafts now need designers to bridge the gap and allow them to compete with products and practices of modern industrialisation. They are very much an economic activity, and the centre of the development process is design and marketing. Craft production cannot be economically viable unless the product is marketable. This is where design intervention plays a critical role, ensuring this viability and matching technique with function. Design and marketing intervention has been a springboard for successful interventions across the country. The embroidered Chamba *rumal*, a languishing craft, where a sensitive interface resulted in a revival of this craft; the *sanjhi* stencils where the paper template used to make the ritualistic *rangoli* is now a well-known craft are only some examples. Craft cannot be static as it must respond to changes in markets, consumer needs, fashion trends and usage preferences. Design and marketing inputs are an important aid to the craftspersons who are removed from their new markets.

Six decades after Indian Independence, crafts remain one of the subcontinent's strongest, yet anonymous influences over modern everyday life. The cultural exchange continues till today, a unique one in which the traditional crafts and craft-traditions of India have been translated into contemporary products and interact with the demands of urban living, resulting in a juxtaposition of ancient technologies catering to a globalised world. Craft has moved ahead — it is not static or crystallised in time nor is it contained; its essence lying in movement and in constant flux. Traditions and contemporary developments meshed into craft production and consumption reveal not only the persistence of memory and adaptability to change but also the impact of India's craftspersons in an interconnected and interdependent world.

Ritu Sethi is the head of Craft Revival Trust.

Artists marvel at the Ganesha idol after embellishing it for Ganapati puja in Bangaluru.

Why Hollywood is Romancing Bollywood

Meenakshi Shedde

One of the things that makes me fiercely proud of India, is Indian cinema. A few facts about it then, straight off the bat. First, India is the largest film producer in the world, with 1,146 feature films in 2007. The US makes about half that number annually, and France only about a fifth. Second, India makes feature films in upto thirty-nine Indian languages and dialects annually (this dropped to twenty-two languages in 2007), which must make it the most diverse cinematic cultures in the world. This must easily beat all the cinematic languages of the European Union — from just one country. But third and most splendid of all, is that India must be the only spot on the entire planet, where Hollywood is small change. Even after operating in India for nearly a century, Hollywood has a crummy 8 per cent of the Indian film market. Very few countries can boast of such a strong national cinema. Imagine, Hollywood's biggest hit in India, *Spider-Man 3*, would scramble to find a place in India's top twenty box office hits!

This says something for Indian cinema, that despite cohabiting with Hollywood in India, Indian films have 92 per cent of the domestic market. On the other hand, Hollywood's stranglehold has destroyed national cinemas worldwide. When French films grabbed 45 per cent of their own domestic market in 2007, it was party time (French films get state support and there are quotas supporting French films on television). In Germany, German film-makers are delighted to have managed even 25 per cent of their own market. Iran and China severely restrict film imports. Korea has been fighting Hollywood with a quota system reserving a minimum number of theatres screenings for Korean films annually. But India is an open market where Hollywood operates freely, and the Indian film industry gets negligible state support. Yet Hollywood, with all its powerful marketing juggernauts, big guns like Steven Spielberg and Tom Cruise, and after dubbing its films in Hindi, Tamil and Telugu apart from English, has managed to capture not even a tenth of the Indian market.

An Indian woman looks at a promotional poster of Hollywood film *Spider-Man 3* at a multiplex in Bangaluru.

(*Pages 61 – 62*) A poster of the Indian movie *Om Shanti Om* which delighted the Bollywood fans even in Berlin (*left*). The poster of the blockbuster *Lagaan* which gathered worldwide acclaim and was India's second prestigious entry to the Oscars (*centre*). As the Indian cinema captures the gaze of the world the Hollywood producers wish to grab 'a bite of the cake'. Warner Bros'. first co-production with an Indian director is *Chandni Chowk to China* (*right*).

Although Bollywood — mainstream Hindi films made in Mumbai — is the most high profile part of Indian cinema, it is barely a fifth of India's total film production. The film industries in Tamil and Telugu are equally strong; we also make films in Bengali and Malayalam, and all of these enjoy fierce loyalty from their audiences.

The truth is that Indians are crazy about movies and music, and simply adore their own films. The masala film formula of mainstream Indian cinema continues unabated. It is a cheerful, nonchalant tutti frutti of genres — romance, action, comedy and suspense, all propelled by high-octane songs and dances shot in various countries — and topped off with a happy ending. Indian musicals are an all encompassing mainstream formula, not a specific genre as in Hollywood. That's because Indian cinema drew its origins from Indian theatre, folk forms and mythologicals, in which song and dance were traditionally part of the narrative. The owners of the early Indian cinema theatres were mostly owners of drama theatres, and in the early days, Indian cinema was, to some extent, filmed theatre. So since its origin, songs and dances have been part of the indigenous Indian film narrative. Whereas in Hollywood, musicals

really grew from the 1930s, essentially as a cheery antidote to the Great Depression of 1929, and it has remained a genre.

For all its improbable narratives, the Indian film industry posted healthy profits of USD 135 million in 2006. And Indian films were globalised half a century before the terms "globalisation" and "cross-over" became common currency. In the silent film era, three famous Indo-German co-productions directed by Franz Osten of Munich — *Prem Sanyas* (*The Light of Asia,* 1925), *Shiraz* (1928) and *Prapancha Pash* (*A Throw of Dice,* 1929) were shown in Europe and India. In the early days after Indian independence in 1947, when India was a socialist economy and had close ties with the former USSR, films particularly those of Raj Kapoor, were popular throughout the USSR. For decades, Bollywood films have been popular across a wide swathe — from Egypt, West Asia, Central Asia and Russia, throughout South Asia, including Pakistan, Malaysia, Hong Kong, Indonesia and Singapore, right upto the Philippines. For a decade now, they have been doing good business in the UK, US and parts of Europe; and mainstream Indian films like Mani Ratnam's *Dil Se* are routinely in the top ten in the UK. Tamil films do good business in West and South Asia, especially

Malaysia, as well. What's more, Bollywood films are increasingly popular on the international film festival circuit: Sanjay Leela Bhansali's *Devdas* was at Cannes, Farah Khan's *Om Shanti Om* was at Berlin, Mani Ratnam's *Yuva* was at Venice and Karan Johar's *Kabhi Alvida Na Kehna* was at Toronto.

While Hollywood offers mainstream films with special effects appealing to the eye, Bollywood offers mainstream, sentimental films appealing to the heart. In fact, romantic fantasies are such a staple of most mainstream Indian films, including Bollywood, that reality is even seen as an unnecessary interloper. Sundered hearts will be reunited at any cost, logic and reason be damned! So, for instance, it is common for spirits of dead people to take rebirth in order to organise happy endings for lovers and this has been depicted in various films like *Om Shanti Om*.

Like Hollywood, Bollywood too uses a broad template that is universally understood across cultures. Its themes draw on the eternal struggle between good and evil, and it underscores traditional family values as they grapple with modernity and globalisation. Nobody watching a Bollywood film in any part of the world can be confused who is the hero, who is the villain, and that the lead pair who is madly in love can't marry because the girl's Papa insists she has an arranged marriage with someone else. In Aditya Chopra's evergreen *Dilwale Dulhaniya Le Jayenge*, another love marriage versus arranged marriage affair, Shah Rukh Khan, the current Bollywood heart-throb spends only one-third of the film romancing the heroine, and two-thirds of the film romancing his future father-in-law, in order to secure permission to marry his daughter. He wants to weasel out that very Indian invention — an 'arranged-cum-love marriage'. The film was such an incredible hit, it has been running in Mumbai's Maratha Mandir theatre since thirteen years. Name one Hollywood film that has run that long. And a lot of the film's fans are seeing the film for the twenty-fifth or forty-fifth time, they know all the songs and dialogues by heart, and the big high is reciting and singing along, in the theatre, in real-time.

Music is not only a traditional element of our entertainment; it is critical to Indian filmmaking economics. Quite often, even if the film flops at the Indian box office, producers recover about a third of the total cost from audio music sales and another chunk from overseas film rights and are home and dry. It is not unusual for

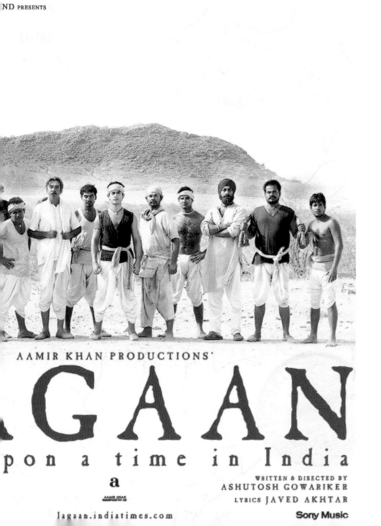

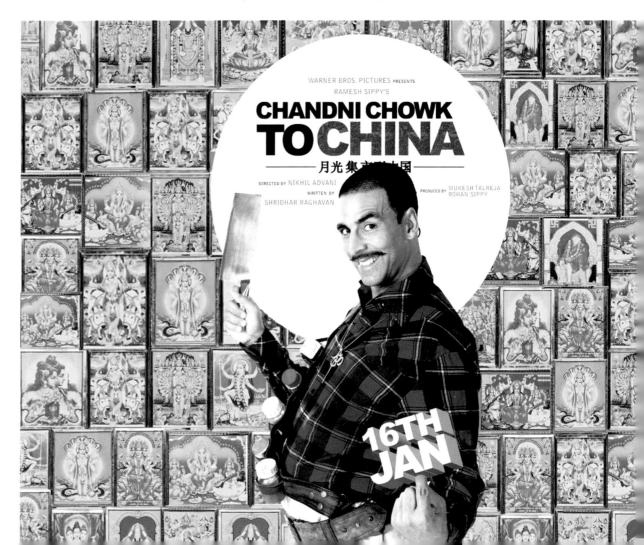

Bollywood producers to raise the entire budget for a film by finalising the stars and music director of the film: the story and script are mere trifles that can be filled in later.

No wonder for Indians, there is no polite way to watch a film: their relation to cinema and music is visceral and expressive. Watching a Bollywood film in an "ice-cream palace of a theatre" in Rajasthan, Baz Luhrmann, director of *Moulin Rouge*, said it represented a seminal moment in his understanding of cinema. The audience was singing aloud the songs in the film, chatting, answering mobile phones, eating, drinking, thoroughly enjoying itself. He said he tried to generate Bollywood's interactive quality when making *Moulin Rouge* which went on to win an Oscar.

Not everybody can handle Bollywood's interactivity, though. Once, I'd taken a Parisian friend to see a Bollywood film at Metro cinema in Mumbai, and she was horrified by the 'live action' in the audience. In the row before ours was a family with three children, who were constantly talking, laughing, eating popcorn and making trips to the toilet. I had to explain to her that for an Indian, going to the movies was like going on a picnic with a movie in the distance. The movie was part of a larger enjoyment of life, not a one point agenda. I realised why she was unable to sit back and enjoy the movie. When I had watched my first film in a Parisian theatre, *Monty Python's Life of Brian,* and collapsed with laughter, everyone glared at me for daring to laugh aloud in a theatre. For the French, cinema halls are like cathedrals. "I'm sorry, but it's really funny", I said in a small voice, but the French remained unmoved.

Indian ways of seeing a film are fundamentally different from the West's, and different cultural resonances can make for some piquant situations. Take a popular Hollywood film like *Titanic,* that was such a big hit globally. A few years ago, I was line-producing a German

An array of hoardings of Indian films — both new and old, seem to be inviting one into the world of Bollywood.

documentary in India. We were shooting touring tent cinemas in Shingnapur village in drought-prone Satara district, in interior Maharashtra. We asked a touring tent cinema owner how the *Titanic* had fared in the district. "We get very poor rainfall here," he said. "Farmers work on such parched lands in the remote interior, they found it hard to believe there could be so much water anywhere, and couldn't be bothered with such strange fantasies. So the *Titanic* sank without a trace." Forget Hollywood, even Bollywood was unreliable business there. The longest running film in Satara, that ran for over a year, was a regional language Marathi film called *Kalubai Navane Chang Bhala* (With the Blessings of Kalubai), about a woman with mother-in-law problems, whose worries are all sorted out after she prays to snake god!

Satara, of course, is an exception. Indian film fans' addiction to the cinema and idolatory of the stars is legendary, if not actually pathological. Politicians shrewdly tap into this mania as the boundaries between reel and real life dissolve, and many film stars are active politicians. South Indian films stars like MG Ramachandran (MGR) and Jayalalithaa in Tamil Nadu, and NT Rama Rao (NTR) in Andhra Pradesh, have ruled as chief ministers and headed political parties for decades. Along with Rajnikant and Rajkumar, these film stars have cult followings that sometimes beat Bollywood cults — and certainly Hollywood film cults. When superhero Amitabh Bachchan was in hospital, the entire nation came to a standstill and prayed for his recovery. When MGR was shot in the throat by a co-star and temporarily lost his voice, thousands of MGR fans observed *mouna vratam* (penance of silence) for his recovery. He won the 1967 election from his hospital bed.

These film stars often played gods in mythological films or Robin Hood style vigilantes bringing justice for the poor, and their fans are their vote banks. On hot summer days, MGR's fans have distributed cool buttermilk for those in the queues at cinema halls, and in the monsoons, they have distributed raincoats and umbrellas. They have donated blood and, with the compensation, purchased tickets for the first day first show of the latest MGR release. They have beaten up journalists who criticised their *thalaivar* (chieftain). They have erected roadside temples to him and conducted puja (prayer ceremony), pouring

The proud DVD collection of an avid German fan of Bollywood.

Indian heart-throb Shah Rukh Khan charms Berlin during a tour in 2008.

milk and honey over enormous cutouts of their star on the day his new film releases. What do fans of Tom Cruise do? They are thrilled to bits if they get his autograph or get to touch his sleeve. Hmm.

While star mania and romantic fantasies have been perennial aspects of Indian cinema, at least the romantic fantasies didn't always enjoy the stranglehold they have had since the 1990s. These Westernised romances emphasising traditional Indian values — cinematic sheep in wolf's clothing — generated huge box office value from non-resident Indians overseas. However, since the pre-Independence era, Indian cinema has tackled social and nationalist themes through the work of film-makers like V. Shantaram, B. N. Sircar, Himansu Rai and others. The 1950s and 1960s were the golden period of Indian cinema, continuing the nationalist theme, but also questioning our legacy and Nehru's vision of a socialist economy, with great directors like Mehboob Khan (*Mother India*), Bimal Roy (*Do Bigha Zamin*), Raj Kapoor (*Awara*) and many others. The 1970s saw the "parallel cinema" emerge, with directors making powerful, incisive films that tackled feudalism, political corruption, injustice, Partition and the exploitation of women through a whole body of work including Shyam Benegal's *Ankur*, Govind Nihalani's *Aakrosh*, M. S. Sathyu's *Garm Hawa* and others.

Meanwhile, arthouse cinema had always had deep roots in regional languages, particularly the communist ruled states of Kerala in South India (in Malayalam) and West Bengal in East India (in Bengali). Since the mid-fiftiess, Satyajit Ray, one of the masters of world cinema, made films mainly in Bengali, that were rooted in his region and culture, yet had universal resonances. Along with other directors, he was powerfully influenced by Italian neo-realism — using realistic themes and non-professional actors — in particular the work of Vittorio De Sica and his *Bicycle Thieves*. His vast oeuvre includes the much loved Apu trilogy *Pather Panchali* (The Song of the Road), *Apur Sansar* (Apu's World) and *Aparajito* (The Unvanquished); *Charulata* and *Jalsaghar* (The Music Room). Other internationally acclaimed Bengali directors include Mrinal Sen and Ritwik Ghatak. The next generation of talented Bengali directors includes Rituparno Ghosh, Anjan Das and Suman Mukhopadhyay. Kerala, too, has spawned great directors such as Adoor Gopalakrishnan, whose films include *Elippathayam* (The Rat Trap) and *Kathapurushan* (The Man of the Story); G Aravindan's *Vasthuhara* (The Dispossessed) and Shaji Karun's *Piravi*. The younger generation to watch out for includes Shyamaprasad, Rajiv Vijayaraghavan, Priyanandanan and Vipin Vijay.

Traditionally, mainstream and arthouse cinemas were not on speaking terms, but they have been dating since the 1990s. This has spawned "the new Indian cinema" that is entertaining, sensitive, thought provoking, sometimes in English, and may not have stars or songs at all. While Rajkumar Hirani's *Lage Raho Munnabhai* was a brilliant mainstream entertainer reviving Gandhi's non-violence in contemporary times, other low budget films like Nagesh Kukunoor's *Dor*, Sagar Ballary's *Bheja Fry* and Ram Madhvani's *Let's Talk* pushed the edge of alternative Indian cinema further. The nationwide multiplex boom with 14,000 screens and smaller theatres, is helping break the romantic stranglehold by making a variety of scripts viable.

But make no mistake: the big bucks come from masala films like *Om Shanti Om* and broad comedies like *Hera Pheri*. And as Hollywood seeks a piece of the action, it has been forced to go *desi*. Most Hollywood majors, including Sony Pictures Entertainment, Warner Bros., Viacom, Disney and Twentieth Century Fox, are now considering producing Indian films by Indian directors in Indian languages. For the first time, Sony Pictures Entertainment produced an Indian film, *Saawariya* directed by Sanjay Leela Bhansali in Hindi, in 2007. The company is doing more co-productions with UTV as well as Eros International. Twentieth Century Fox co-produced Mira Nair's *The Namesake* with UTV. Warner Bros. is co-producing a slew of films starting with Nikhil Advani's *From Chandni Chowk To China* in Hindi. Foreign studios are also co-producing and outsourcing animation and special effects to India, which has high level expertise that is relatively cheaper. Disney has inked a deal with Bollywood's biggest producer Yash Raj Films, to produce animation features; Warner Bros., Sony Pictures

Shopkeepers selling kites with the pictures of admired Bollywood actors posted on them during the kite festival of Uttarayan in the town of Khambhat, Gujarat.

Entertainment and Viacom are tying up with other Indian animation companies.

With the new generation of film-makers and the commercial interest of the international community, there is a renewed confidence in Indian cinema. That breezy confidence might also explain its appeal to white, non-traditional audiences overseas.

Still, one can't help feeling that the day Indian and Chinese cinema — with the biggest emerging markets — start

co-productions, we can bring out the prayer beads for the future of Hollywood in India.

Meenakshi Shedde, freelance journalist, critic and curator, is former Assistant Editor of The Times of India. *Winner of the National Award for Best Film Critic, she was on the FIPRESCI Critics' Jury of the Cannes, Berlin and Venice festivals. She is also advisor on Indian cinema to the Cannes, Berlin, Venice and Toronto film festivals. She contributes to media worldwide, including* Variety *(US),* Cahiers du Cinema *(France),* Sight and Sound *(UK),* DNA *(India) and has written for the book* Au Sud du Cinema. *She has directed the short film* Looking for Amitabh, *and line-produced five international documentaries shot in India.*

A shot of recent Hindi movie *Ghajini* at a theatre in Connaught Place, New Delhi.

(*Pages 71 – 72*) The varied moods of the Indian cinema of yester years.

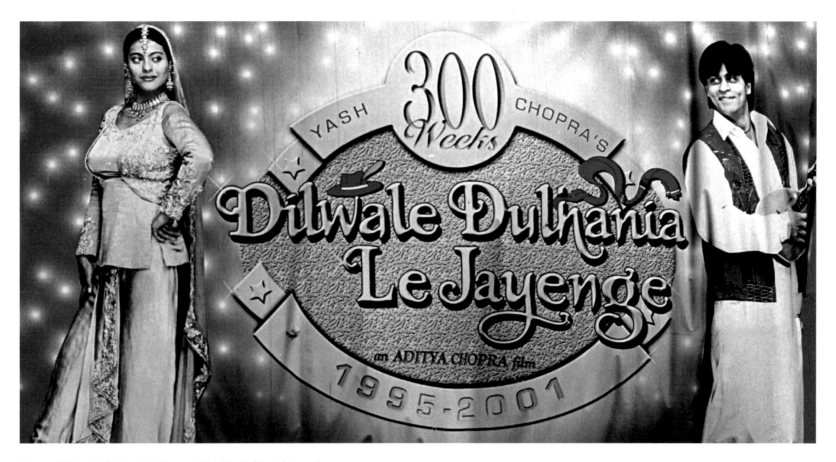

Poster of *Dilwale Dulhania Le Jayenge*. The Hindi film is being shown at the Maratha Mandir cinema hall for the past thirteen years.

Contemporary Indian Literature

Pratik Kanjilal

When you think Indian literature, you probably think of the Booker Man. People from elsewhere get the Man Booker. Indians are more fortunate. They have a walking, talking, writing Booker Man. Salman Rushdie has received three versions of the Booker for the same book, *Midnight's Children*. He got the plain vanilla Booker in 1981, the Booker of Bookers in 1993 and the Best of the Booker in 2008. For most readers outside of India, Rushdie Version 3.0 is the face of Indian literature.

The reader who penetrates beyond Rushdie could reach Vikram Seth, Amitav Ghosh, Arundhati Roy, Amit Chaudhuri and Upamanyu Chatterjee. Further on in the gloaming, the truly intrepid might happen upon wandering bands of lesser-known authors, mostly diaspora expats, all writing in English. For most fans of Indian literature, that is land's end. Beyond lies the unknown, clad in impenetrable darkness.

It's a pity they stop there, because the darkness conceals a literary supercontinent. Indian literature in English is only a promontory jutting out from a vast mainland that the world is now discovering. India speaks in about 2,000 tongues and writes in fifty languages, which shows substantial publishing activity. There are about 15,000 publishing houses, which push out 70,000 new titles every year, and only a quarter of this volume is in English. Thirty-five languages have print media, seventy-two are taught in schools, 146 are broadcast on the radio and films are produced in fifteen languages. The country has twenty-four official languages in which government business can be transacted. Each has a unique script, grammar, vocabulary, literary history and represents a unique culture. It's enough to put Babel to shame. By way of comparison, the European Union, which represents a whole continent, has only twenty-three official languages, all written in Roman script.

A modern bookstore in New Delhi with a café lounge offers a diverse
range of Indian as well as international titles.

So if you're only reading Indian literature in English, you've put your hand to the tail of the elephant in the fable of the five blind men. You are totally unaware of the magnificent animal the tail is attached to. The elephant, meanwhile, is not amused by your ignorance. If you keep fiddling with its tail instead of standing back and admiring its imposing presence, it just might get irritated enough to try and stomp you.

Back in 1986, India was guest of honour at the Frankfurt Book Fair, the trendsetting event of global publishing. Everyone involved remembers how she was shamefully ignored. "Your delegates went back disappointed," recalled Nobel-winning German novelist Günter Grass. "They knew all about us. I remember I'd go to a decrepit old house in Calcutta, I'd be ushered into the library by an elderly gentleman and find all the Western classics — Rilke, the Russians, English literature. India has been enormously interested in Europe and in 1986, that interest was not reciprocated."

To be fair, it wasn't entirely the fault of the hosts. They found their guest of honour remote, uncommunicative and incomprehensible, the perfect stereotype of the inscrutable oriental. As one German publisher said, "Your publishers remained trapped in their own languages, in the ghetto of incompetence. Ventures to promote regional literatures flopped."

In 2006, India was again guest of honour at Frankfurt. This time, there was no ignoring her. Kiran Nagarkar's *God's Little Soldier*, hot of the press in Germany, was the centre of attention. Dancers Astad Deboo and Navtej Johar performed to sellout crowds. Wherever you went, India was in your face. You couldn't flip the TV remote without an Indian mug staring back at you. Flip, and you were watching Aishwarya Rai in *Devdas*, speaking flawless Deutsch. Flip again, and it was Günter Grass and Amitav Ghosh discussing the Indian National Army and the Battle of Kohima. Flip again, and you were watching manic *Börsengurus* (stock analysts) hustling on Dalalstrasse (Mumbai's Dalal Street). Flip again, and there was an anchor posing that eternally intriguing question: What are the Ambanis up to now?

India aims to achieve total literacy which is bound to result in phenomenal growth in Indian publishing industry.

(*facing page*) A woman listens on headphones to an introduction to the Indian language of Hindi at the International Book Fair in Frankfurt, Central Germany.

Between 1986 and 2006, everything had changed. India had become a tiger economy, the only Asian democracy to grow at breakneck speed. Also, Europeans had realised they had a lot to learn from India, the original multicultural country, which has successfully weathered the very issues which now plague their newly variegated society. In fact, with its Hindu-Muslim divide, India is a Petri-dish version of the Huntingtonian clash of civilisations which the world believes it is now facing — if such a thing can exist at all.

In the twenty years between the two book fairs, India's cultural ecosystem too had changed almost beyond recognition. Frankfurt 2006 was attended by writers who were largely post-Independence. Their themes were contemporary, global and quite accessible to the Western readership. For instance, Kiran Nagarkar's special interest is the interplay of religion and politics, something that Europe is painfully aware of after a spate of terror bombings. Twenty years earlier, the continent had been dominated by authors who had experienced the freedom struggle or lived under the shadow of the Fabian socialism that followed. There was very little common ground that a Western reader could find with their world.

At the same time, the world at large had changed and was better prepared to understand India. The concerns which form the work of a Dalit writer like Namdeo Dhasal may seem inaccessible to foreign readers because they are rooted in India's unique caste system. But a Western reader who knows of the Black civil rights movement will find them quite familiar. Said Grass at the fair: "It isn't like before. Now, the German readership would welcome Saadat Hasan Manto's modernism, for instance."

More importantly, Indian language writing had come out of the ghetto. Today, there is no serious publisher in India without work in translation on its list. Despite decades of work by the National Book Trust (especially its Adan Pradan project) and the Sahitya Akademi, the national academy of letters, translations used to linger on the back shelves of bookstores, waiting to be remaindered. These titles are now at the forefront of mainstream publishing in India.

Until the nineties, translation from the Indian languages into English was largely the preserve of a few creative people and

HINDI LANGUAGE

अ आ क ख ग घ च छ ट ठ त थ

Hindi

Students reading in a quiet corner of the JNU library, New Delhi.

academics like A.K. Ramanujan. Translated titles did not exactly sell like hot cakes and most work appeared under the aegis of the Sahitya Akademi. The Akademi churned out books and translated material that appeared in *Indian Literature*, the journal which it had established in 1957, originally to chronicle its activities. But these publications were meant principally for academia and litterateurs, not the lay reader. The Akademi's priority was to put Indian literature on the record, not to popularise it. All that changed when publishing firms got into the act and secured the attention of the reading public.

India has had the experience of translation from very early times. The first dated, printed book in the world, published in China during the T'ang dynasty in 868 AD is a translation from Pali, the language from which most of the modern tongues of North India trace their descent. That was six centuries before the Gutenberg Bible, but there's a copy in existence, discovered in the Dunhuang Buddhist cave complex on the Silk Route. Here, in 1907, the archaeologist Sir Aurel Stein found a perfect Chinese copy of the *Vajracchedika Prajnaparamita Sutra*, better known to neo-Buddhists as the *Diamond Sutra*. Interestingly, the colophon of the sixteen-foot scroll states that it was printed for free public distribution. Even eleven centuries ago, it seems, Asia understood the power of translation to convert.

In the early and middle twentieth century, translation between the Indian languages played a major role in holding together the country, which had never been a single political entity until Independence. Half a century ago, people down south were completely familiar with Bengali literature, which then held a pre-eminent position, because novelists like Bankim Chandra Chatterjee and Saratchandra Chatterji, apart from Rabindranath Tagore, were routinely translated and published in local languages. Nationalist and modernist ideas travelled freely and widely thanks to translators, whose role in forging the national temper is all but forgotten now.

The Indian languages themselves have been instrumental in holding South Asia together. Most of our neighbours share a language with us. No discussion on Bengali literature is complete without reference to Bangladesh, which was born out of a civil war for the recognition of Bengali as the national language. Contemporary Tamil literature is incomplete without taking into consideration Tamil writing from Sri Lanka, which has starkly documented the horror of the civil war in progress there. All writers working in Nepali don't live in Nepal. Some are quite at home in India — just as Nepal's first president, who took office in 2008, is of Indian origin. And it is impossible to speak of Urdu literature, such as the work of Qurratulain Hyder and Kaifi Azmi, without mentioning Pakistan, where Urdu is the national language. No wonder track two diplomacy is held in such high esteem in this region, riding on cross-border exchanges in music, theatre, cinema and literature.

Now, translation is helping India reach out to cultures beyond the subcontinent. Rather than trying to lure seasoned Indian writers in English — none of whom have favoured Indian houses, except Amitav Ghosh — publishers have turned to the vast body of literature in the Indian languages which is just waiting to be discovered. Texts being translated range from the Upanishads, the core post-epic teachings that began to be compiled in the middle of the first millennium BC, to contemporary popular literature like Shankar's Bengali hit *Chowringhee*, inspired by Vicki Baum's *Grand Hotel* (which was itself a translation from the German *Menschen im Hotel*, 1929). Translators are attempting to render poetry, which is notoriously resistant to translation, sometimes with excellent results. The most interesting success in recent times is *Says Tuka*, a rendering of the seventeenth century Marathi Bhakti poet Tukaram by Dilip Chitre, himself a poet who writes with equal facility in Marathi and English. And meanwhile, the children of the diaspora are being raised on the epics in the form of English comics.

This explosion in translation activity is helping to lay to rest an acrimonious class war in Indian letters. Politically, the Indian literary world is divided into two camps: those who write in English and those who write in the Indian languages. The first scornfully — and a little fearfully — regards the second as a bunch of benighted natives stuck in the past, ignorant of the world at large. The second camp disparages the first as a bag of dandified, deracinated human coconuts, brown on the outside, white on the inside.

Rootless, inauthentic people with no idea of where they have come from, and therefore no idea of where to go to. There is some truth in the allegations that each party levels at the other. *Desi* writing tends to be closer to the ground it springs from, while English writing favours diasporic themes and locations.

Until the seventies, the two camps were nodding acquaintances. The *angrez* lot had a world readership, but the Indian language crowd sneered that they had a bigger readership right here at home. In fact, they enjoyed rock star status among their fans and regarded

the human coconuts as the exotic pygmies of the world of English literature, with even other colonials like V.S. Naipaul towering over them.

After the publication of *Midnight's Children* in 1981, the two camps were not on speaking terms. For the *desis*, not to have access to a world readership was tolerable, but to live like paupers

while the English-wallahs made millions was beyond endurance. Through the eighties and nineties, few international conferences on Indian literature failed to degenerate into a catfight about why expat writers in English were paid so much to produce so little of abiding value while the genuine, autochthonous artisans slogged it out in the heat and dust of the home country, wrote great literature and died in obscure penury. It is a tribute to India's non-violent traditions that no one put out a *supari* contract on Salman Rushdie before the Ayatollah could launch his *fatwa*.

Who exactly was to blame for this crazy feud? Not the *angrez* writers, who were just doing their thing, writing for a global readership. Certainly not the *desis*, who were writing for the local readership as they were supposed to. The problem was that through the latter half of the twentieth century, there was no culture of translation in Indian publishing which could bridge the divide between the two. Academics and litterateurs were connecting just fine on the international networks, but the readership remained divided as if by a guillotine.

Despite the current boom in Indian translation activity, it is still an uphill battle because the world publishing industry is in an unusually conservative mood. Freshly corporatised and rather obsessed with the balance sheet, it is disinclined to favour experimentation. Besides, retailing is now as standardised as an automobile production line. If a bookseller is not sure which shelf an experimental title goes on, it will probably be rejected. Try to imagine a Borders manager in New York wondering where to place a novel by a Dalit writer railing at Brahminical society in a Maharashtra village while betraying a partiality for West Bengal-style Maoism, and you'll get the problem. You might say that the Indian industry is waiting for international publishing to catch up with it. People in this region have been writing from the twenty-seventh century BC, going by the evidence from the Indus Valley, and have a lot of things to say that do not fit neatly into Western categories. That is the beauty of Indian literature. Unfortunately, in the international marketplace, it is also its handicap.

A roadside book shop which stocks all from religious books to old titles of Hindi literature.

Contemporary Indian Literature | 80

Meanwhile, writing in English continues to thrive, having moved on from the pioneering generation of Mulk Raj Anand, R.K. Narayan, Nissim Ezekiel, Dom Moraes, Arun Kolatkar, Keki Daruwalla, Gieve Patel and others, whose pursuit was high literature. Publishers have been building on the ground prepared by early practitioner-proselytisers like Jayanta Mahapatra, who publishes a literary journal, *Chandrabhaga*, and Adil Jussawalla, who edited the path-breaking *New Writing in India* in 1974. Sales and readership figures are quite small by world standards, but current publishing makes up for that in variety. There's a lot of classy writing from unknown bylines appearing in various journals but the Indian writer in English is no longer a litterateur by default.

Chetan Bhagat's surprise hit *One Night @ the Call Centre* taps into the contemporary work culture of the IT and BPO boom in India. Chick lit is booming, cashing in on the increasing confidence and independence of young urban women. Titles do entertaining send-ups of traditional Indian society, where sex is still something to be kept under wraps and love inevitably leads to marriage, predicted by the family astrologer and presided over by the family priest. The Indian graphic novel has carved out a niche of its own. And children's writing, which has always been a hot industry in the Indian languages, is now picking up in English, fuelled by the needs of parents who have let their mother tongues slide but don't want their kids growing up only on foreign writing.

So, there is no dearth of variety in English, but it's nothing compared to the supercontinent

Nai Sadak in Chandni Chowk, Delhi is one place people would throng to get their sack full of books and also save their pockets through attractive discounts.

that translation represents. Big publishers have barely begun to explore its beaches and ports. The vast hinterland with its rainbow of tongues is still almost unknown, but stories of its riches have begun to colour the imagination like the travellers' tales that brought the Europeans to India five centuries ago and changed the map of the world forever.

Such is the variety of the Indian literary traditions that it would be madness to attempt a definitive reading list or a synopsis. But here's a little sampler to give you some idea of what's going on, selecting one major language from each cardinal point of India.

North/ Hindi

Hindi, once derided as the language of the under-cultured, now has a widely dispersed readership and is a major literary language. The story of modern Hindi fiction begins with Babu Devki Nandan Khatri's *Chandrakanta*, a wild yarn rife with romance and intrigue set in a fictional fortress modelled on Chunar Fort near Varanasi. Published at the end of the nineteenth century, it is regarded as the first novel in Hindi and remains wildly popular. Neerja Guleri adapted it for television in the mid-nineties and a movie is in the pipeline starring Amitabh and Abhishek Bachchan. Intriguingly, there have been reports from Uttar Pradesh villages of Chandrakanta, the heroine of the novel, being worshipped as a goddess.

Ever since Munshi Premchand introduced realism, Hindi literature has been enormously inventive. Having gone through romantic (the *Chhayavadi* of Jaishankar Prasad, Sumitranandan Pant and Mahadevi Varma) and realist experimentalist movements (the *Nai Kahani* of Rajendra Yadav, Mohan Rakesh, Nirmal Verma and Kamleshwar), it is now embraced by a wide variety of writers, from mainstream but experimental voices like Krishna Baldev Vaid, Krishna Sobti, Mridula Garg, Mrinal Pande and Uday Prakash to vehicles of Dalit outrage like Om Prakash Valmiki. Bhisham Sahni is well-known all over India, especially for *Tamas*, a Partition story which was adapted into a very successful teleserial. Notable poets

A view of the Daryaganj weekly book bazaar in Delhi which gets converted every Sunday into a book lovers' festival.

include Shrikant Verma, S.H. Vatsyayan, who wrote under the pen-name Agyeya, Kedarnath Singh and Kunwar Narain. The younger writers include Manglesh Dabral and Alka Saraogi.

South/ Malayalam

Contemporary Malayalam writing is about as intense as it gets and will appeal to fans of the psychological novel. The modern pathbreaker was Vaikom Muhammad Basheer (1908 – 1994), a freedom fighter of the Bhagat Singh era who was jailed during the

salt *satyagraha* and then started a revolutionary journal. With a warrant out for him, he escaped from Kerala and wandered all over India and places in Asia and Africa, supporting himself by taking on unexpected identities, including those of shepherd, fortune-teller and ascetic. Basheer returned to Kerala after seven years on the road and started a literary career amid tremendous financial adversity. A lively innovator honoured by the Padma Shri, he broke the mould of

Malayalam literature and introduced the use of living language, as it is spoken by common people.

The best known contemporary writer from Kerala is probably Kamala Das, fiction writer and poet in Malayalam and English, and pioneering feminist. M.T. Vasudevan Nair is a powerful realist who, apart from the Sahitya Akademi award, has also won the National Film Award for best screenplay five times. Others who are available in translation include O.V. Vijayan, K. Ayyappa Panicker, Thakazhi Sivasankara Pillai, K.N. Panikkar, N.S. Madhavan, M. Mukundan, Paul Zacharia, K. Satchidanandan, Sara Joseph and Balachandran Chullikad.

East/Bengali

Bengali had a literary head start over most Indian languages. Buddhist mystic poetry containing Bengali forms dates from the eighth century. In modern times, Bengal was the centre of British power and nationalist resistance to it, and was the crucible of a literary ferment. Rabindranath Tagore and Saratchandra Chattopadhyay remain widely known even among people who have never read them because decades after their passing, their works still inspire blockbuster movies from Bollywood. But beyond them are hundreds of writers, poets and playwrights, literally far too many to mention. Authors range from classic names like Bibhuti Bhushan Bandyopadhyay (author of *Pather Panchali*, which was made into a celluloid classic by Satyajit Ray), Tarashankar Bandyopadhaya, Aabu Sayeed Aayub, Rajshekhar Basu, Annadashankar Ray, Ashapurna Debi, Jibanananda Das, Bishnu Dey and Banaphul to contemporary masters like Mahashweta Devi, Subhash Mukhopadhyay, Sunil Gangopadhyay, Shakti Chattopadhyay, Nabaneeta Dev Sen, Shankho Ghosh and Joy Goswami.

Bengali literature is one of the few language genres to have ventured into science fiction. If you just want to test the waters of Bengali rather than diving in at the deep end, the science fiction stories of the Oscar-winning film-maker and author

A monk reads a sacred Buddhist text printed in the traditional Indian *pothi* style at Bodh Gaya.

Satyajit Ray, which have been translated, serve as a good entry point. Many believe that one of them inspired Steven Spielberg's *ET*.

In 1962, Ray wrote a sci-fi story titled *Bankubabu's Friend*, featuring a creature remarkably like Spielberg's extraterrestrial. In 1967, he wrote it up as a script for a Indo-US co-production titled *The Alien*, backed by Columbia Pictures and starring Marlon Brando and Peter Sellers. However, Ray found that his script had been attributed largely to his Hollywood agent, who had approached him through Arthur C.Clarke. Then Brando dropped out and the project foundered, though Columbia expressed interest repeatedly through the seventies and eighties. When *ET* was released in 1982, both Ray and Clarke saw clear similarities with Ray's script. Read the original story for yourself and you'll be kind of convinced, too.

Spielberg has denied any connection, but Ray always believed that *ET* would not have been possible without reference to his script, photocopies of which had been floating around in the Hollywood community. For the record, Ray did not make a penny from the project.

West/Marathi

Marathi literature traces its roots to the early medieval period, when a number of saints doubled as poets and writers. With a newspaper of its own as early as 1835, modern Marathi is marked by an extremely vibrant theatre scene. Until recently, a very large number of Bollywood actors had a background in theatre and even after they found success on the screen, they continued to perform on stage. Vijay Tendulkar is Marathi's — and India's — most celebrated dramatist and has been translated quite well. In fiction, good starting points for exploration are Bhalchandra Nemade, Vinda Karandikar, Namdeo Dhasal, Kusumagraj and Vishnu Sakharam Khandekar. From these authors through Vilas Sarang to the

A man engrossed in reading in natural environs at Ahmedabad.

new generation represented by poets like Hemant Divate and Sanjeev Khandekar, Marathi literature presents a long tradition of innovation and experimentation.

In Maharashtra, innovation has been accelerated by a little magazine movement, which made its presence felt in two waves. The first came in the 50s and the second is in progress right now. For instance, Divate's magazine *Abhidanantar* is incubating new schools of poetry, including one which is strongly influenced by the language of the digital age. Incidentally, like Bengali, Marathi has a strong tradition of science fiction, the noted astrophysicist Jayant Narlikar being the best known author. Marathi women writers were early movers — Kashibai Kanitkar (1861 – 1948) was the first major woman novelist. And the language boasts of an unusually high number of bilingual litterateurs, like the poets Arun Kolatkar and Dilip Chitre.

As stated earlier, this brief introduction barely scratches the surface of Indian letters. If you're inclined to delve deeper, sahitya-akademi.gov.in, the website of the national academy of letters, is the best jumping-off place. It lists prize-winning writers from all the nationally recognised languages, whose names should top any reading list.

Pratik Kanjilal is publisher of *The Little Magazine*. His honours include the Sahitya Akademi Translation Prize (2005) and the New York University Prize for Hyperfiction (1998).

A person absorbed in reading a sacred text in a cave in Idar, a historical and religious town about 100 kms north-east of Ahmedabad.

Curried Away

Amit Dasgupta

'Indian' food and cuisine is the global flavour these days. However, because of the huge diversity in cuisine in India, the use of a generic term like 'Indian' cuisine is completely misleading, as it seeks to generalise where it simply cannot and, in fact, should not. North to South, East to West, the variations are incredible. Indeed, to even categorise the diversity in terms of 'North' or 'South' is itself a misnomer. In a city like Calcutta or Kolkata (as it is now known) for instance, there are several different types of cuisine available, which are all typical to the city. These range from Bangla or Bengali food to Goan cuisine, Anglo-Indian food to the Afghani and Muslim food, the vegetarian cuisine of the long resident Marwari community to Kolkata's own variation of Chinese and Continental cuisine to the distinctive 'club cuisine' and equally distinctive 'street food'. This would be true as well for Bombay or Mumbai (as it is now known) and so many other cities in India.

Indeed, the unique characteristic of 'Indian' cuisine is the range and variety between adjoining states, cities and even, districts. Climate and religion, customs and geography have had their own impact on food habits and cooking styles. The cooking medium can change depending on the kind of regional cuisine one is looking at; while Bengali cuisine would tend to predominantly use mustard oil, certain kinds of cuisine in southern India would opt for coconut oil, for instance. There is also a vast range of vegetarian food in India with unique differences; Jain vegetarian cooking, for instance, which the Jain community refers to as 'pure vegetarian food' is without garlic or onions and any root vegetables; Jain cooking also does not use eggs and many Jains would avoid using dairy products. Similarly, in comparison to vegetarian preparations in Punjab, Bengali vegetarian cuisine tends to use minimal spices. Indeed, Bengali vegetarian cuisine or *niramish* resolutely shuns garlic and onions, and relies on minimal use of spices. As opposed to, of course, that wonderful Punjabi (or North Indian) preparation of roasted aubergine (*baigan*

An expert chef tosses roti in the air before
putting it on the *tandoor*, Indian clay oven.

In a roadside shack in Mysore a vegetable seller makes his own
version of a departmental store as he stores heaps of ginger,
chilli, cucumber, pumpkin, etc. with pride.

ka bharta) in which the use of sautéed onions and garlic and ginger are simply mandatory!

With the growing popularity of vegetarian food, especially among the younger generation in North America, it is fascinating to see how the non-resident Indian community has spread the message of different kinds of Indian vegetarian cuisine, among which *sattvik* cooking is being touted as 'food for the soul' ("Eat healthy to think and live healthy"). *Sattvik* food is essentially 'healthy food' in that it avoids food items which are highly processed and where there is use of chemicals and pesticides. Organically farmed fruits and vegetables would be the core ingredient of *sattvik* food. Additionally, contrary to fast (or junk) food, *sattvik* food is cooked over a slow flame and is never overcooked. Each ingredient used is identified for its influence on physical and mental well-being. *Sattvik*, which broadly translates into 'pious' is completely vegetarian but, interestingly, unlike the Jain cuisine, ginger as an ingredient is used in such preparations.

Vegetarian food is integral to Indian cuisine and India's vegetarian traditions are ancient. References to it may be found in early scriptures, both Hindu and Buddhist. The principal objective behind Indian vegetarian cooking is to take advantage of the medicinal qualities of fruits, vegetable and spices.

Apart from the fact that there are considerable variations in the style of cooking in different parts of India, it is also important to point out that within India, various religious communities had freedom to cook their own particular kind of cuisine, even if it went against the beliefs of another religious community. To give an example, let us recall that India is a predominantly Hindu country and yet there are some parts of India where beef is served and that these 'beef recipes' are handed down over generations, as indeed is the fact that pork recipes — anathema to the Muslims, who are over 130 million in India — are also handed down, generation after generation. Interestingly, both beef and pork recipes are also very much part of 'Indian' cuisine. Cuisine in India, thus, not only reflects its huge regional diversity and uniquely tolerant and abiding secular spirit but also the influences over several centuries borne out of invasions and occupation.

Another common misperception is the reference to all Indian main courses as 'curry'. It is not clear as to how this came about. It is speculated that the English word 'curry' is derived from the Tamil word *kaikaari* or *kaari,* which is essentially a kind of vegetable preparation cooked in *kaari* leaves with spices and coconut. Some say that since the prolonged British sojourn in India started in Bengal, where there is a highly popular and wonderful Bengali preparation called *torkari,* which is a vegetable stew; it could have been the inspiration for the British to create the word 'curry'. Of course there is also the story about the good English girl, far removed from her British upbringing, who suddenly discovered that her native cooks were using what they were referring to as a *karai,* or wok, for their cooking and that led to the birth of the term 'curry'.

Whether this was the kind of deductive logic the British used to coin the term 'curry' continues to be a matter of speculation. But, it is a fact that the word is widely used today to describe *all* Indian preparations. In 'Indian' cuisine, however, the word 'curry' is used to refer to preparations with a sauce or gravy, as opposed to a dish which is essentially dry and without the use of several spices. Of course, there are some Indian recipes where the sauce or gravy is reduced considerably so that it only coats the main ingredient; this kind of reduced gravy preparation is called *bhuna,* which roughly translated would be 'roasted' and is essentially a Mughlai preparation made with meat; it is eaten best with Indian bread (rotis or *rumali*s) but goes equally well with hot steaming rice with a dash

India boasts of almost 200 varieties of banana. Incense sticks placed by the shop owner at a roadside banana shop reflect India's deeply entrenched religious ethos.

of clarified butter or ghee. Interestingly, there are superb *bhuna* preparations from other parts and cuisines of India, such as Kerala, which reinforces the point that the 'Indian cuisine' is difficult to type-cast.

Briefly then, 'curry' is basically a preparation that uses different kinds of spices that go into the making of a gravy of a particular kind; 'curry powder' is, thus, a blend of spices and is used in the preparation of a sauce to cook a particular kind of Indian food.

Curry Powder

Ingredients

- 4 tbsp coriander seeds
- 2 tbsp cumin seeds
- 2 tbsp fennel seeds
- 2 tbsp fenugreek seeds
- Dried chillies (to taste)
- 5 dried curry leaves
- Chilly powder to taste
- 1 tbsp ground turmeric
- Salt to taste

Dry roast the above, except chilly powder, turmeric and salt for a few minutes, stirring constantly. The spices will darken but take care that they do not burn. You will get a distinct and rich aroma. Remove from fire and allow it to cool. Put the roasted spices in a mixie and grind to fine powder. Alternatively, use a pestle and mortar to grind the spices.

Separately, mix chilly powder, ground turmeric and salt. Add the ground roasted spices to the mixture.

It is also worth mentioning that more often than not, especially in the Western world, what is usually known as 'the Indian cuisine' is essentially North Indian cuisine, especially tandoori, along with curry-based preparations (both vegetarian and non-vegetarian) because of its understandable appeal and popularity. Indeed, usually a menu order that is considered to be very 'Indian' would be a plate of *tandoori chicken* to start with, rotis and naan as accompaniments, a dal (possibly *makhni* or yellow dal), a mutton or chicken *rogan josh* or curry, *palak paneer*, *raita* and a sweet dish (*gulab jamun* or if available, 'Indian ice cream' – *kulfi*). All in all, this is actually quite an enjoyable and wholesome meal.

Years ago, I recall driving through Germany and stopping by a remote town. What amazed me and my family was the totally unexpected, and hugely welcome, presence of a Chinese restaurant with an extraordinarily good menu, including preparations that the non-Chinese would not normally opt for. In other words, the non-Chinese who were frequenting the restaurant (which could take around forty persons) were quite happy trying out what they were not 'traditionally' used to as 'Chinese cuisine'. I learnt afterwards that there was in the vicinity, a popular Indian restaurant too that served tandoori and was 'doing well'.

Interestingly, what is increasingly happening in continental Europe (it happened years ago in the UK and in North America) is the sudden proliferation of Indian restaurants; unfortunately, most of these restaurants serve truly distasteful food but for unsuspecting Europeans, who have never tasted 'the real thing', this experimenting with 'other cultures' is part of their current psyche. Some attribute this to the new-found interest in Bollywood; this is quite possible given the fact that Bollywood films are now on prime time TV in several European countries and dubbed in the local languages. However, I would be more inclined to suggest that there is a growing and new-found interest and openness among Europeans to 'other cultures' which possibly explains the entry of films, music, fashion, literature, art, culture and cuisine that is foreign and perhaps, even exotic and alien to Europe.

Madhur Jaffrey's seminal TV programme and accompanying books were the first major foray in the UK, not only as an introduction to Indian cuisine but indeed, to the spectacular diversity of India. Despite Madhur Jaffrey and several other efforts, the knowledge of what exactly is 'Indian cuisine' has understandably

A fruit shop selling watermelons in front
of Cubbon Park, Bangaluru.

differed from country to country. To some extent, this has been 'diaspora driven'; in the UK and in Northern America, the persons of North Indian origin far outweigh those from other parts of India and furthermore, tend to be far more entrepreneurial, especially in the restaurant business. In most of East and South East Asia, on the other hand, 'Indian' food in its many avatars is actually known and appreciated. This is not only diaspora-led but also greatly influenced by the cultural and religious ties that have historically bound India and the region civilisationally. Large numbers of persons of Indian origin in East and South East Asia are not only from northern India but also from southern India and as such, the variety of 'Indian' cuisine available in the region is considerable.

There is, thus, considerable interest in 'Indian' cuisine and given the fact that it is only partially known, as a purely business or commercial proposition, a good 'Indian' restaurant has huge potential, especially since mediocre Indian restaurants appear to be enjoying roaring business with gullible and unsuspecting food experimenters!

In the UK, the interest for 'Indian' *khana* (food) is such that, in several supermarkets, it is possible to find sandwiches with *chicken tikka masala* and other variations. In short, 'Indian' food has really caught on there. It is, however, a pity that, the cooks in most of the cheaper and neighbourhood 'Indian' restaurants are essentially from Bangladesh many of whom have little, if any, knowledge or expertise in cooking 'Indian' cuisine. Indeed, 'Indian' restaurants have proliferated quite simply because 'Indian food' sells in the UK, as opposed to other South Asian cuisine. 'Indian' cuisine has established itself, just as much as Japanese or Chinese or French or Continental food has. I have always wondered why these mediocre Bangladeshi-run restaurants in the UK insist on serving 'Indian' food when they could actually do quite well by serving genuine and hugely palatable, simple Bangladeshi home food! This is, however, not true in North America where the 'Indian' cuisine tends to

Mega feast at the Aranmula Temple in Kerala, during Krishnashtami (the birth anniversary of Lord Krishna). The feast usually has over one lakh people participating and the menu includes around forty-one items of traditional Kerala cuisine.

essentially have a North Indian bias and is far more authentic simply because most of the cooks, being from northern India itself, happen to be well-versed in the native cuisine. Furthermore, their entrepreneurial acumen has helped them identify wholesome 'Indian cuisine' as a profitable business USP.

Like much of international cuisine, the 'best' Indian food is what is served at home; hotel or restaurant cuisine, however tasty, tends to be rich and oily and grossly over spiced, apart from being

avoidably overpriced. Home food is simple, wholesome, nutritious and well-balanced. It is well-accepted in India that the best outside-home food is served in *dhaba*s or road side rustic restaurants; indeed, *dhaba* cuisine has enjoyed a formidable reputation of its own and people will travel great distances to try out particular recipes that some *dhaba*s have developed a penchant for. The recipes in this

article are based on home-cooking and as such, might lack the flair of restaurant flourish but, I'd bet my last penny, taste-wise they could take on the best the restaurants can offer!

In the remaining part of the chapter, I will attempt to 'work' on a 'menu' for a non-Indian (read: predominantly 'Western') audience. To some extent, this is primarily because Indian cuisine simply does not follow the principle, so prevalent in the cuisine of several countries of being 'course-based'. For instance, it does not provide for 'starters' and 'soup' before the main dish. It is important to mention that much of Indian food, whichever region we are looking at, is essentially a kind of *thali* (all food served in a platter) experience. Indeed, even if the food is not served on a *thali*, it would be fairly typical for all the preparations to be brought to the table simultaneously. Of course, as is typical of anything Indian, there are differences. For instance, if you happen to go for a wedding dinner — especially in eastern India and to a Bengali wedding, in particular — food would normally be served on banana or plantain leaves (if the traditional service is followed, which is usually customary) and then, the different items on the menu would come in 'installments' or sequentially or 'course wise'.

Soup, as is known in the West or in Chinese and Japanese cooking, is essentially alien to 'Indian' cuisine. In some parts of southern India, however, it would be quite traditional to begin a meal with what is known as 'drinking *rasam*' (which is served hot in small stainless steel glasses) but that is more as an appetiser than as a wholesome starter. The *mulligatawny soup*, which is an English or Anglo-Indian adaptation of an Indian preparation, is quite popular. On a cold and winter night, this is wholesome and nutritious, and could indeed, be a complete meal in itself, much like the Irish stew. However, with minor adaptations and reduced quantities, it can be converted into a highly recommended first course.

Mulligatawny is the anglicisation of the words *mullga*, literally meaning 'pepper' and *tanni*, which literally means 'water'; in other words, 'pepper water'. It is a humble lentil based soup meant to be served hot. It is essentially a non-vegetarian preparation but

Turmeric, which is sometimes also called as Indian saffron, has been a major Indian spice since ancient times and is still a favoured ingredient for most Indian recipes.

can very easily be made into a vegetarian preparation by removing the shredded chicken and replacing the chicken stock with vegetable stock. This is also meant to have a spicy (chilly hot) tang to it, which may naturally be adapted to taste.

Nevertheless, it needs to be said that this is, indeed, a time-consuming preparation if one wants to get it 'right'. It is well worth the effort though, for when 'right', it is simply a magnificent innovation. This is also a preparation that has continued to evolve and there are several variations, including among international chefs, of what might be the 'authentic' preparation or on modifications thereof. In cooking, it is possibly best to go by individual tastes rather than authenticity, especially if one is cooking for friends and family.

Mulligatawny Soup

Serves: 4 – 6 persons
Ingredients

- 2 tbsp salted or clarified (ghee) butter
- 2 stalks of celery chopped
- 1 carrot, peeled and chopped
- 1 large onion (preferably red), peeled and chopped
- Chillies, red or green, according to taste
- 5 cups of stock (chicken or vegetable)
- 1/4 cup cooked red lentil to make 4 – 6 servings
- Half an inch of peeled and chopped fresh ginger
- Salt and pepper to taste
- 1 tbsp curry powder
- Half a cup of coconut milk
- 1 tbsp of cooked rice per serving
- 1 tbsp of shredded cooked chicken per serving
- Fresh lemon juice and coriander leaves for garnishing

Heat a non-stick deep dish, put in the butter when hot, add chopped celery, carrot, onion, and pepper in the butter at a low heat until the onion is translucent. Add curry powder and stir till mixed; after a few minutes, add the stock and bring to a boil. Reduce heat, cover and simmer for around 10 – 15 minutes till the celery, carrot and onion are cooked; add salt, chillies and freshly ground pepper to taste. Let it cool, add fresh ginger and strain. The strained soup may be returned to the pot and put on low heat.

When ready to serve, put a tablespoon each of lentil, cooked rice and shredded chicken (drop the chicken for the vegetarians) in each individual serving soup bowl and add the hot soup. Garnish with a dash of coconut milk, a generous squeeze of fresh lemon juice and finely chopped coriander leaves.

The second course could consist of both vegetarian and non-vegetarian preparations, depending on, quite naturally, the guests you are inviting. In any case, given the huge repertoire of vegetarian preparations in 'Indian' cuisine, it is always a pleasure to include vegetarian preparations that are quite simple and easy to make. Menus, in terms of the second course, could either be two tandoori preparations, one vegetarian and the other non-vegetarian, or some other preparations with a common vegetarian item.

A tandoori preparation should, normally, be cooked in a tandoor, which is a clay oven, heated on high heat by charcoal and used for baking bread and roasting meat. However, since not everyone has a tandoor, adaptations have been made and while a precise 'real thing' might not be possible (especially the smoky flavour) through an oven, a reasonable second-best is surely possible. The true test of a tandoori preparation is to ensure that the meat (or the vegetarian item) is succulent and has not dried up.

Corn on the cob which in its Indian avatar would be sprinkled with salt and lemon juice or tamarind chutney.

Tandoori Chicken and Tandoori Paneer

Serves: 4 – 6 persons
Ingredients

- 4 – 6 pieces of chicken (with skin removed); preferably leg and joint; it is also possible to use boneless chicken cut into large pieces, though 'traditional' *tandoori chicken* preparations would be with bone; if using, boneless chicken pieces, 1 ½ inch thick cubes would be ideal; poke the chicken all over with a skewer or make incisions with a knife.

- Paneer comes in the form of bricks if bought from an Indian shop; cut into cubes so that each cube is at least a one inch thick piece; 2 – 3 pieces per person is required; if the guests eat both vegetarian and non-vegetarian food, look at a maximum of two paneer pieces per person along with the *tandoori chicken* piece, if with bone, or around two boneless chicken pieces.

- Butter or cooking oil

For marination

- Beaten or whisked yogurt sufficient to coat all the chicken pieces adequately with some left for pouring over.
- 3 – 4 tbsp of ginger-garlic paste
- Chilly powder to taste
- Tandoori masala paste (this is now readily available in 'dry' or 'wet' form; either can be used)
- Mashed raw (green) papaya paste (to be used as a tenderiser for the chicken)
- Salt to taste

For serving

- Lettuce
- Onion rings
- Lemon juice

Marinate the chicken with all the ingredients, making sure that each piece is well-coated. (Note: The paneer does not require the raw papaya as a tenderiser as it is ready to eat.) Leave in the refrigerator for at least four hours and preferably overnight. Before cooking, bring it back to room temperature.

Put a *karai* on high heat; once hot, turn to medium; add butter or cooking oil and then, chicken pieces (or paneer pieces) taking them out one at a time, so that all the marinade does not come off. Add to *karai* and toss so that chicken pieces (or paneer) does not burn and ensure that the gravy does not stick to the *karai*. After around 8 – 10 minutes for the chicken and 6 – 8 minutes for the paneer, turn off heat.

Meanwhile, in an oven friendly dish, put a little of the marinade and spread evenly. Place the chicken/paneer items neatly and add marinade, making sure that each piece is well-coated but at the same time, ensuring that not all the marinade is used. Prior to doing all this, make sure that the oven is put on pre-heat at around 200°C. Let the oven be on for at least 10 – 15 minutes before putting in the chicken or the paneer pieces. Check after 10 minutes and turn the pieces over and baste with remaining marinade.

It is not a bad idea to consider using cut pieces of green pepper which could be added with the chicken/paneer while roasting in the oven.

Serve on a bed of lettuce along with onion rings and a generous squeeze of lemon juice. Normally, this is best served with mint chutney, for which, a sprig of fresh mint leaves, double the quantity of fresh coriander leaves (cilantro), ginger, garlic cloves, green chillies to taste, salt and freshly ground pepper should be ground in a mixer; thereafter, the mixture should be mixed with a bit of natural yogurt and served as an accompaniment.

There are other preparations that one could go in for, leaving the tandoori behind or working in combination. The most common preparations are in terms of 'chops', which are essentially potato encased preparations that are fried and variations can be found in different parts of India.

Delhi, particularly Old Delhi is a gastronomic feast especially during
the periods of festival. This man and his family sell a type of vermicelli
called *sewaiyan*, near the Jama Masjid.

Potato Chop

Serves: 4 – 6 persons
Ingredients

- Oil for deep frying
- Bread crumbs
- 2 – 3 large sized potatoes
- Salt
- Chilly powder to taste
- 1 tsp ginger-garlic paste
- Finely chopped coriander (cilantro) leaves
- Dry roasted and powdered spices:
- Red chilly powder
- Cinnamon stick
- Black pepper corns
- Fenugreek seeds
- Black mustard seeds
- Coriander seeds
- Cumin seeds
- Cloves

*For filling

Vegetarian

- Crumbled paneer
- Parboiled and chopped beetroot
- Parboiled and chopped carrot
- Roasted and chopped peanuts

Non-vegetarian

- Minced meat

For serving

- Lettuce
- Tomatoes
- Cucumbers
- Onions
- Whiped yogurt
- Coriander leaves
- Chopped green chillies

Boil the potatoes, peal skin and mash along with salt. Mix and mash well till there are no lumpy bits of potato and the salt has blended well. Keep aside and prepare filling.

For vegetarian fillings, take crumbled or finely chopped paneer (North Indian cuisine) or a combination of beetroot and carrot that is parboiled in advance and thereafter, chopped in fine pieces but not mashed (Bengali cuisine); add some dry roasted (plus chopped) peanuts for taste. Some adaptations that could be considered, since cooking is essentially a matter of experimentation, is to do the stuffing with pureed spinach which has been garnished with chilly. Alternatively, the spinach and the crumbled paneer could be put together as the filling. For the very popular North Indian preparation of *aloo tikki*, no fillings are used and it is a delightful potato item. Several variations are possible, including using a soft cheese (like *Amul*, for instance) or the delightful *aloo methi ki tikki* (potato and fresh fenugreek leaf patties) or the Hyderabadi vegetable *shikampuri kebab*s.

For non-vegetarian fillings, minced meat is usually the norm. A portion of chicken or mutton (goat meat**) mince is cooked to tender and thereafter, passed through a mixer to mash it to a fine paste. This is, then, used as a stuffing. Several variations are possible: tuna fish or crab meat from a can.

Thereafter, prepare small cakes (ensure that the vegetarian items look different from the non-vegetarian items), roll in bread crumbs and deep fry. Serve on a bed of lettuce leaves and with chopped onions, tomatoes and cucumber in whipped yogurt, garnished with chopped coriander (cilantro) leaves and finely chopped green chillies.

*For hundred grams of filling (vegetarian or non-vegetarian) the total quantum of spices should not exceed one teaspoon.

**Most of the red meat consumed in India is mutton or fresh goat meat; the majority of butchers are Muslim and the meat is cut to halal norms, though it is possible to find butchers who are not Muslim, in which case, the goat is not butchered as per Muslim traditions and is called *jhatka* as opposed to halal. Since goat meat, as the expatriate Indians normally know it, is difficult to find in Europe and in North America, adaptations are made of many traditional goat meat recipes, using young lamb from which the fat is removed. While many claim that this is a great 'second best', I have my reservations! It is essential to increase the quantity of spices to take away the typical lamb smell.

Indian cuisine is wholesome and nutritious because a proper Indian meal served at home would be balanced. While there are many Indians who are vegetarian and there are a large number of excellent vegetarian preparations, much of Indian cuisine tends to be non-vegetarian with at least two vegetarian items as accompaniments to the 'main course', along with a dal or thick (the consistency is a personal preference) lentil broth or 'soup' consumed as an accompaniment. In Bengali cuisine, for instance, fish preparations are almost obligatory with every meal and at least one meal (usually for dinner during weekdays and at lunch time on holidays) would also have a meat preparation.

With regard to vegetarian food, since this chapter aims at demonstrating the variety and diversity in Indian cuisine — both vegetarian and non-vegetarian — Jain recipes, as far as vegetarian cuisine is concerned, might be an interesting preparation to consider. Earlier I have referred to the number of ingredients that are a complete no-no for the Jains, such as root vegetables — ginger, garlic, onions, etc., actually, even potatoes! Many would consider a potato as a 'mother of all veggies' and I truly cannot fathom a German meal as being complete without a potato preparation!

It would not come as a surprise if established cooks wonder as to how a recipe without most of the above items might be edible. The idea is to be open to recipes from other cultures and quite frankly, the Jains and their cuisine has been with us for several centuries. Indeed, when a lunch or dinner menu is prepared, it is well worth including a Jain preparation, not only because it adds a distinctively new kind of flavour, but also because Jain cuisine is very healthy. Interestingly, Jain cuisine has 'substitutes' for several items that they do not use and which are considered 'normal' in other preparations.

Dry Green Peas and Raw Banana/Raw Papaya/ Green Pumpkin *subzi* (Jain preparation)

Serves: 4 – 6 persons
Ingredients

- 1 cup frozen green peas, defrosted and washed
- ½ cup of chopped tomatoes (blanched, de-skinned and de-seeded is recommended)
- 2 large raw bananas or half a green papaya or 250 gms of green pumpkin [Note: If you are using raw bananas, which are a standard 'substitute' in Jain cooking, get two thick bananas, around 5 – 6 inches in size; with a sharp knife, cut the skin off completely and then, cut the banana into cubes; similarly, if you are using green papaya, cut it into half, remove the seeds and then, remove the skin and cut it into cubes; with regard to the green pumpkin, some people enjoy eating it with the skin but you could very well remove it with a knife, which would also reduce the cooking time. The green papaya and the green pumpkin tends to cook much faster than the raw banana and will also soften considerably during cooking, while the raw banana will stay fairly firm.]
- Red chilly powder (as per taste)
- 4 fresh green chillies, slit in the middle
- ½ tsp of *amchur* (mango powder)
- ½ tsp turmeric powder
- ¼ tsp of cumin and mustard (black) seeds
- 1 tbsp of garam masala
- Pinch of asafoetida
- Pinch of sugar
- Salt to taste
- 1 bay leaf
- 2 cups of beaten fresh yogurt
- Chopped coriander leaves for garnishing
- 2 tbsp oil

Heat oil in a pan. Add bay leaf, cumin and mustard seeds; when they just begin to sizzle, add a pinch of asafoetida and sugar quickly, add the chopped tomatoes; stir to ensure that the spices do not burn; allow to cook for half a minute;

add turmeric powder and mix well; after half a minute or so, when the tomatoes begin to soften, add little water and mix and then cover for 30 seconds; the tomatoes should become like puree. Add the chopped vegetable that is being used (raw papaya, raw bananas or green pumpkin); mix well so that the cubes of vegetable are well-coated; cover and cook for a while, adding a little water if necessary; once the vegetable is cooked, add the green peas, *amchur* powder, salt and the beaten yogurt; allow to cook, mixing well on reduced flame. The liquid should dry up and this should be a reduced gravy that does not stick to the pan but coats the vegetable pieces. Serve after sprinkling the garam masala. Garnish with chopped fresh coriander leaves and fresh green chillies.

Garam Masala: This is now readily available in all Asian stores that have Indian spices; only traditionalists or gourmet cooks would actually make their own garam masala. This masala is a mixture of dried red chillies, cinnamon, curry leaves, coriander and cumin seeds, black pepper corns, cloves, fenugreek seeds, black mustard seeds and chilly powder. It can either be used for making the gravy and thus, cooked or it may be sprinkled dry after the cooking.

The repertoire of Indian vegetarian cooking is considerable and in several households, adaptations are made, possibly because good cooks experiment! More often than not, these are based on the seasonal vegetables that are available.

Perhaps, one of the classic terms in 'Indian' cooking is the use of the word *andaaz*, for which it is difficult to find an exact translation: the closest, quite possibly, is *intuition*. It is quite normal for recipes that are handed down from grandparent to mother to children for *andaaz* to be an important element of how much spices or salt or whatever to put into the food! I've seen my mother put her hand into the salt jar and take out what turned out to be the 'right' quantity or measure: she said that she knew 'instinctively' whether it was too much or too little; much of the recipes that come handed down from mother to child are 'instinctive' or *andaaz*-based, in terms of salt and the quantum of spices to be used. It is, therefore, a credit to all those who have been writing about 'Indian' cuisine that they have actually given accurate measures of the quantum of spices to be used. Most cooks would agree that the problem really is with

A roadside *dhaba* in Sonepur, Bihar.

salt and as the maxim runs: it is easy to deal with less salt, it is quite impossible to handle excess salt in the cooking!

Five-minute Green Beans
Courtesy Deepa Dasgupta

This is a magnificent dish from Karnataka and easy and quick to cook.

Serves: 3 – 4 persons
Ingredients

- 250 gms of (stringless) green beans; ends cut off and then cut into half inch pieces or into smaller pieces, as required.
- Pinch of asafoetida
- 2 cloves of large garlic crushed
- 2 dried red chillies
- ½ tsp of mustard seeds
- Salt to taste
- Shredded fresh coconut
- 1 tsp oil

Heat oil in a wok, when hot, add crushed garlic, dried red chillies and stir; add mustard seeds and asafoetida and immediately add beans; stir and ensure that the beans are constantly mixed; add salt. Serve with shredded fresh coconut (optional but recommended).

It is reasonably difficult to classify the different repertoires of vegetarian cooking in India. In northern India, popular vegetarian cooking tends to be rich (in the use of both, spices and oil) but in several other parts of India, vegetarian cooking is much less spicy without compromising on taste. This does not, however, mean that tasty North Indian preparations tend to be calorific and 'rich' and thus, need to be avoided by the weight conscious. Indeed, one of the highly popular North Indian vegetarian preparations (*baigan ka bharta* or mashed barbequed aubergine) is also a very healthy preparation and superbly tasty to boot! Generalisations on 'Indian' cooking are, therefore, quite misleading.

The vast repertoire of Indian vegetarian cooking is quite extraordinary and before I move on to some popular and easy-to-cook non-vegetarian preparations, I cannot but share the recipe of one of my favourite vegetarian dishes. I first tasted it when my mother-in-law prepared it and since then, it has been one of my all time favourites. *Taambli*, which is essentially a coastal Konkan or Mangalorian preparation, can indeed be made using different items as a base; in the recipe I reproduce, spinach is the base, though I am informed bottle gourd also works.

Taambli
Courtesy Deepa Dasgupta

Serves: 4 persons
Ingredients

- Bunch of fresh spinach; washed, chopped, boiled and cooled. This might not be necessary in many places as it should be possible to find the spinach in near pulverised form in supermarkets.
- Take the same quantity (by volume) of desiccated coconut and put it in a bowl.
- Green chillies to taste
- 1 tsp cumin seeds
- ½ tsp tamarind paste
- 1 tbsp clarified butter
- Salt to taste

Fry green chillies and cumin seeds in clarified butter (or ghee); take out into a mixer and add the boiled spinach, desiccated coconut and tamarind paste; blend to a fine paste. Put on fire and add salt. Serve hot. This is, in fact, a dish that works, even when served cold.

Let us move on to the non-vegetarian. Like vegetarian cooking, the non-vegetarian preparations in India are vast in terms of their sheer range. But, let us consider some 'classics' — both little known and popular — from different parts of India so as to demonstrate the diversity in preparation and taste. Of course some other 'classics' would be left out such as those

Mango, the king of Indian fruits is also India's one of the most famous export to the world.

wonderful preparations that come from the north-east of India, such as a delightful prawn preparation cooked in a bamboo tube or the spectacular Bengali preparation of prawns slow cooked in a coconut shell! Alas, it is difficult to do justice all that is so wonderful in 'Indian' cuisine in a single chapter and so, what we will do is to start with Kerala with a delightful chicken preparation — a pepper chicken and then, move on to the very popular *rogan josh,* which is a North Indian preparation of mutton/lamb and from there, journey on to Kolkata for the traditional mustard fish and then, zip down to Goa for the delectable *Goan prawn curry.*

Pepper Chicken: Kerala Style
Adapted by Deepa and Amit Dasgupta

We have usually enjoyed this as a great 'snacky' appetiser rather than as a main course. However, it can be had as a 'precursor' to a regular main course.

Serves: 3 – 6 persons

Ingredients

- 6 – 12 chicken drum sticks (2 per person), with incisions
- Ginger-garlic paste, with the ginger on a 3:1 ratio vis-à-vis garlic; gently massage the paste into the chicken taking care to push the paste where incisions have been made.
- Generous sprinkle of crushed black pepper (this is a pepper hot dish)
- 2 dry red chillies
- 2 pods of crushed garlic but not made into paste. Mix well with the chicken. Toss the mixture in 2 tbsp of dark soya sauce.
- 3 tbsp oil

Heat oil to high heat, add dry red chillies and pods of crushed garlic, add chicken drumsticks stir and cook on high heat for around 10 minutes, stirring continuously and then, turn to low heat. Generously sprinkle crushed black pepper from pepper mill and make sure that the chicken is well coated on both sides; before serving, add crushed black pepper again.

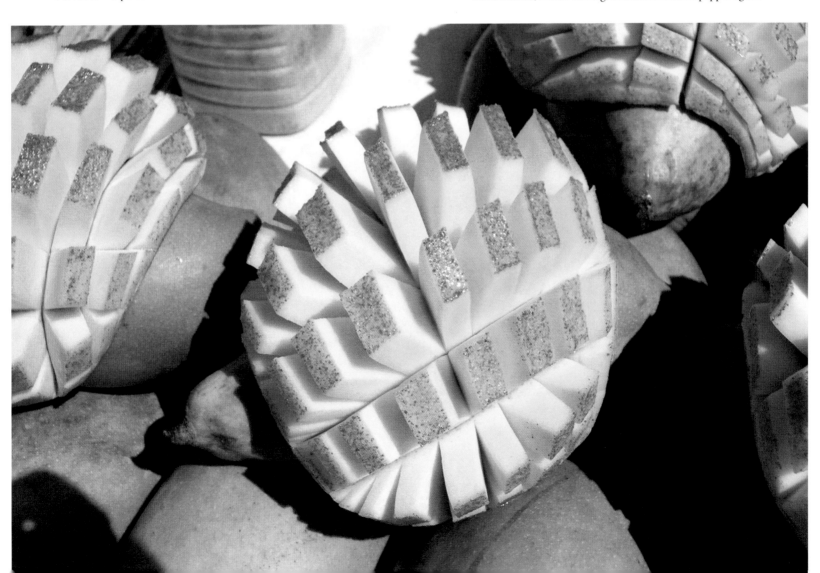

Rogan Josh

This is a Mughlai preparation. The word rogan refers to a preparation in clarified butter, while josh refers to passion; this is always a meat preparation. The principal ingredient is fresh goat meat or mutton, which is not readily available in most countries. As mentioned earlier, lamb meat has its own distinctive smell as indeed does fresh goat meat. Normally, those who are used to goat meat or mutton would find lamb meat rather strong in terms of smell while cooking. Adaptations are accordingly made in recipes to counter this 'smell' while preparing goat meat preparations substituted by lamb meat.

It is also important to point out that when Indians purchase goat meat which incidentally is always sold fresh, they would take an assortment of pieces of the meat, including some with bone. The butcher would split the bone through the middle so that during the cooking process, the juices and the marrow would get an opportunity to 'interact' with the spices. It is not uncommon to find Indians keeping the bones aside so that they might chew on them after the meal or dig into for the marrow! While choosing lamb meat, it is important to keep this in mind. Lamb meat tends to be meatier and it would be easy to get boneless lamb meat; however, for a *rogan josh* preparation, it is essential to have bone, including pieces that are taken from the rib cage.

This is, beyond doubt, a fabulous preparation in terms of the many spices it uses and blends and is thus, a preparation where the sheer aroma appetises!

Serves: *3 – 4 persons*
Ingredients

- 750 gms lamb/fresh goat meat (with bone) cut into pieces
- 3 black cloves
- A stick of cinnamon
- A large bayleaf
- 4 tsp of fennel powder
- Crushed black pepper

(*facing page and opposite*) Women enjoying spicy Indian street food in Chandni Chowk, Delhi.

- Salt to taste
- 2 small pieces of cardamom
- ½ cup beaten yogurt
- 2 tbsp oil

For marination

- 2 tsp of ginger paste
- 1 tsp of chilly powder
- Half a bowl of fresh yogurt to completely coat the meat.
- Mix all the ingredients with lamb pieces and set aside for an hour.

For serving

- A pinch of saffron stirred in milk

Heat oil and add black cloves, cinnamon and bay leaf; stir and add lamb/mutton pieces and fry till mutton starts to turn brown, stirring continuously. Add fennel powder, crushed black pepper and salt to taste and stir.

Reduce heat and add cardamom and beaten yogurt; stir till the preparation boils; add water, if required. Cook covered till meat is tender (preferably use a pressure cooker).

Serve with a pinch of saffron stirred in milk.

Shorshay Maach or Mustard Fish
Courtesy Amit Dasgupta

This is a hugely popular Bengali fish preparation and every household has its own particular recipe. The basic ingredients, however, remain more or less the same though there is a debate as to which fish is best suited for this famous preparation; some would say *hilsa,* which is a very bony fish with a fabulous and distinctive taste, while other would say that a *rohu* (carp) would happily be a good enough substitute; I belong to the latter school, much as I love *hilsa.*

Serves: 4 – 6 persons
Ingredients

- ½ kg rohu fish
- 1 tbsp turmeric powder
- Salt to taste
- 4 tbsp mustard seeds
- 3 tbsp poppy seeds
- ½ tsp nigella seeds
- A bay leaf
- Green chillies to taste, slit in the middle
- 2 tbsp oil

For serving

- Steamed rice
- Mustard oil
- Green chillies

Take *rohu* fish and gently massage it with turmeric powder and salt and leave aside for 15 – 20 minutes. As regards the cut of fish, I would recommend the stomach of the fish as the bones are larger and easier to negotiate; Indians eat with their hands and that makes it much simpler to handle bones but if you are using a fork and spoon/knife, the stomach portion would be easier than other parts; alternatively, I've had reasonably good results using a filet of a firm fish (like cod) cut into pieces; salmon works superbly as well, but the delicate scent of the salmon would be overwhelmed by the strong mustard flavour (unfair on salmon, I would say, but a good choice otherwise).

Meanwhile grind mustard (black) and poppy seeds; these days, mustard is available in powdered form and 2 tbsp of mustard powder may be taken and beaten in a couple of teaspoons of full cream milk; thereafter, a teaspoon of paste of poppy seeds may be added to it.

Heat oil; add nigella (cumin) seeds, bay leaf, slit green chillies, a dash (half a teaspoon) of turmeric powder and half a cup of water after the above spices sizzle; add fish and salt to taste.

Let it cook for a few minutes covered; remove cover and add the mustard and poppy seeds mixture. Cover and cook till fish is done. Garnish with slit green chillies. Sprinkle a dash of mustard oil. Serve hot with steamed rice.

Much as this a favourite among Bengalis, the scent and taste of mustard (both in terms of paste and fresh mustard oil) is acquired; my wife, for one, is yet to get used to it; for authentic Bangla cuisine, the mustard oil is highly recommended and Bengali friends will swoon and recall their mother's cooking immediately but, quite frankly, you could happily give the mustard oil a miss!

Goan Prawn Curry
Courtesy Amit Dasgupta

This is an absolutely magnificent preparation, simple to make and yet, amongst the most popular Indian prawn recipes. The Bengali prawn *malai curry*, which is a masterpiece by itself, comes only as a poor second to this simply superb preparation. There are quite a few variations and I recently came across one which includes lady's finger or okra in the recipe but that did appear to be a trifle excessive in terms of both imagination and experimentation.

Serves: 4 – 6 persons
Ingredients

- 1 kg large prawns, cleaned and de-veined; keep aside with a little salt gently massaged.
- Dry roast 1 ½ tbsp whole coriander seeds, 1 tbsp cumin seeds and 10 – 12 whole black peppercorns taking care to see that they do not burn; pulverise fine in a grinder.
- Take out in a bowl and add 2 tsp (or to taste) of red hot chilly powder and 1 tbsp of kashmiri *mirch* or chilly powder (which gives a lovely reddish colour but is not chilly hot) and 1 tsp of turmeric powder; mix all ingredients with a spoon.
- Keep aside 2 tbsp of grated fresh ginger and the juice of 6 cloves of (pulped) garlic; mix together for a ginger-garlic paste.
- 2 medium sized (red) onions finely chopped

Paan eaten after a heavy meal not only helps digestion but also leaves behind a most pleasing and refreshing after-taste on the palate.

(*Pages 109 – 110*) Royal food is served in containers that move on a toy train spread on a huge table at Laxmi Vilas Palace, Gwalior.

(*Pages 111 – 112*) Tourists enjoy their food with local music at a beachside pub at Anjuna beach, Goa.

- 1 even tsp of tamarind paste
- ¾ litre of coconut milk
- Salt to taste
- 2 tbsp oil
- Water

For serving

- Boiled rice

Put the ground spices in a bowl along with the mixture of red chilly powder, kashmiri *mirch* and turmeric powder and add 2 – 3 tsp water and mix well; add ginger-garlic paste and another spoonful of water and mix well till you have a fine aromatic thick paste; set aside.

Heat oil in a pan over medium heat, add the finely chopped onions and fry till translucent; add the spice paste and stir fry for a few minutes; add half a litre of water and let it simmer and cook covered for 10 minutes;

add tamarind paste and pour in the coconut milk, give it a generous stir and add salt to taste; simmer for a few minutes. Add prawns, stir gently but continuously till prawns curl up and turn opaque. Prawns do not take time to cook and one needs to be careful not to overcook prawns. Serve hot with boiled rice.

A chapter on Indian cuisine would not be complete without, at least, a reference to Indian sweets, which like all of Indian cooking, is vast and diverse in its repertoire. Different regions have their own speciality. Bengalis are known for their sweet tooth and claim that Bengali sweets are second to none! Much of the Bengali sweets tend to be *chhena* or fresh cottage cheese-based. On the other hand, much of North Indian sweets are deliciously rich and liberal in the use of nuts.

Sweets are part of the Indian tradition and would be distributed freely as part of a celebration (birthdays, success in school or college examinations or a victory in elections or even

in a game) and always on an auspicious and festive occasion. Indians are happy to celebrate and sweet shops do good business. It is also quite normal for an Indian to greet complete strangers with a sweet to express bonhomie and the fact that the stranger is welcome.

Interestingly, for Indians, sweets are such an integral and normal part of their cuisine that the sequence of its consumption is not always clear! Most Indians would not necessarily end a meal with sweets, though Bengalis would invariably do so. In some parts, sweets would be consumed at tea time. Hot *jalebi*s for breakfast, for instance, is to die for! The Bengali *mishti doi* or sweet yogurt is an excellent end to any meal. Since much of Indian sweets taste good only if they are fresh, a substitute if fresh sweets are not readily available is to fall back on the 'king of mangoes' — the alphonso. When in season, it is possible to get it fresh; otherwise, the tinned

version is usually available at most Asian stores, given the huge demand for the fruit. Served with vanilla ice cream, this is a simple and quite delectable end to any good meal.

The addiction to Indian food can be a lifetime experience. The discovery of the subtle and different flavours can be slow and deeply rewarding. Cuisine becomes a sort of window to the greater world of India's unique diversity. There are many who have been swept off their feet and fallen in love with 'the Indian experience'. I gather, in a sense, they were simply *curried* away!

Amit Dasgupta is a serving Indian diplomat who enjoys cooking.

State of Indian Sports:
A Glass Half Empty or Half Full

Harpal Singh Bedi

It was often said, mockingly or in jest that India, a one billion strong country has yet to produce an individual gold medal winner in the Olympics. All that somehow changed at the 2008 Beijing Olympics as India picked up her first individual gold medal and then, two bronzes. Quite frankly, India went with little expectation especially since she failed, for the first time, to qualify for hockey but as the news of the gold medal came in, the nation went into a state of frenzy and expectations soared.

India has never aimed to become a major sporting power, primarily because her priorities have been on socioeconomic issues and as a result, much required funds were never put into sports. In such a scenario, India's sporting achievements take on quite another meaning.

While deriding Indian sports, the comparison is often done with smaller and much poorer countries; it is often pointed out that since Independence, India has won twelve Olympic medals in fourteen games, while Belarus has won fifteen at Athens Olympics 2004 alone! *New York Times* commenting on Indian sports once wrote that though the demands of development in the third world require priorities other than sports, countries like Tanzania, Kenya and Ethiopia, in comparison, have produced world champions. And other poor or small nations, such as Zaire, Zambia and Uruguay, have at least qualified for the World Cup soccer tournament. But no Indian has won an Olympic (gold) medal in an individual event since India won independence.

Indian passion for cricket is such that children playing cricket in the alleyways makes up for a common sight. Here they indulge in the game outside Red Fort, Delhi.

It further noted, "In light of India's achievements in increasing agricultural production, scientific work and in lifting life expectancy since Independence, the poor performance in sports is not deemed so serious. Nevertheless, it is clear that at least among the urban elite, there is a hunger for a real sports hero."

India's sports achievements have also been severely hampered by dietary realities. Furthermore, India has not been able to create a genuine sports culture. Employment and thus, income generation has been the main issue before youngsters. Family pressure on children is to study and do well and thereby, to try and get a job as early as possible. Sports have accordingly been seen as a leisure activity and a waste of valuable time.

Another possible reason behind the poor health of Indian sports is that India has essentially become *cricket centric* and, as a result, other sports disciplines have either totally lost out or relegated to the background. Indeed, barring cricket, sports in the country has never been taken seriously as it is not seen as a viable career choice.

There is no doubt that cricket has emerged as the number one sport in India and on a scale of one to ten, the discipline is likely to occupy eight slots leaving the remaining two for either golf, tennis, hockey or soccer. Indeed, many would argue that India is essentially a one-sport nation.

"If you are a sportsman, you have to be a class above the rest," said former Indian Hockey captain Pargat Singh. A recent study by a chamber of commerce Assocham further strengthens this belief. "With the exception of the money-spinning game of cricket, a majority of India's urban youth is disinclined in taking up sports as a career and prefers jobs in sectors like finance, retail and IT." Indeed, sports has failed to lure urban youth as a career prospect, with only 30 per cent of the youth from Delhi, Maharashtra, Karnataka, Punjab, Haryana and Uttar Pradesh opting for a career in sports that too, preferably in cricket. This trend is likely to be emulated by the rural youth, as well, with more and more of them opting for cricket as it is perceived as a sport of, "quick and high earning as against hockey, football and archery."

According to Assocham President Venugopal Dhoot, factors for this negative response among youth from major states include lack of corporate sponsorships for games like boxing, athletics, hockey, football, archery, lack of marketing and awareness campaign and huge corporate money garnered by cricket and golf players. As per statistics available, over 68 per cent of sponsorship and advertisement goes to cricket while the rest is divided among other sports.

It is also relevant to mention that things appear to be changing, albeit slowly. Today, there is a conscious effort being made to encourage participation in sports activities. Rural and tribal youth from Orissa, Punjab, Chhattisgarh, Haryana, Jharkhand, Kerala, Goa, North-Eastern states and Uttarakhand are encouraged to opt for a career in sports and are offered employment opportunities in the railways, state government departments, public sector undertakings and corporate houses if they do so. Success in sports has also resulted in out-of-turn promotions and financial incentives.

Regrettably, however, barely 10 per cent of the country's youth have access to sports infrastructure. This critically and negatively impacts on the growth of sports as a career option amongst them.

While it is true that India has not achieved international recognition in sports, there has been active interest and involvement in sports activities, especially in rural areas, as a form of leisure. As a net result, it bears mentioning that in a huge, diverse, multicultural and democratic society, such as India, sports has played a positive role in providing a sense of oneness, unity and national pride.

It might also be interesting to note that, in the early years, sports in India has essentially been a middle and lower middle class phenomenon. Before and immediately after Independence, some former maharajas or royal families took interest in sports but that patronage vanished with the passage of time. Very few

Milkha Singh of India leads French star Abdou Seye to the finish line of
the 400 meters at Fontainebleau Stadium in Paris.

industrialists or politicians (exceptions are there) have shown any serious involvement in games in the formative years. Indeed, the list of illustrious sportspersons who have done the country proud since 1947, more than 90 per cent belong to lower or middle strata of the society. It is these people, who came from humble backgrounds and united the country. They gave their best under trying conditions without economic support. They were not bound by the barriers of religion, caste or language and every achievement of theirs in the international arena was lauded profusely by all Indians. Indeed, it would not be an exaggeration to say that sports has achieved what no other sector of the society has been able to achieve. Sportspersons from humble background rose to become national icons, defying all barriers. In the process, sports emerged as the biggest leveler in a society divided by both caste and class.

Kasabha Jadhav a lowly ranked armyman won India's first individual medal, a bronze, at the 1952 Helsinki Olympics. Similarly, Milkha Singh, a *havaldar* in the army became the legendary "flying Sikh". P.T. Usha, who came from a humble background, became a household name. Archer Limba Ram, a stone cutter from a village in Rajasthan, represented the country at the 1988 Olympics and the Asian Games. An unheralded tribal girl from the North-Eastern state of Nagaland, Mary Kom, hogged the limelight as a pugilist when she performed an unprecedented golden hat trick at the World Championships. Sportspersons from the North-Eastern states of India have performed commendably: midfielder Talimeran Aao from Nagaland was the vice captain of 1948 Olympic Indian football team, Baichung Bhutia is among the topmost soccer players in the country today, Gorkha boxer Padam Bahadur Mal won the gold medal in the lightweight category at the 1962 Asiad.

Caddie turned professional Shiv Shankar Prasad Chowrasia earned the distinction of winning the highest pay cheque on Indian soil when he claimed the Indian Masters Golf in 2008 in Delhi. Most caddies, who come from poor backgrounds, have struck it rich on the domestic circuit.

M.S.Dhoni, from a lower middle class family in Jamshedpur,

Sania Mirza (top) and Mahesh Bhupathi on their way to winning the Mixed doubles final match at the Australian Open Tennis Championship in Melbourne, Australia.

(*facing page*) Yuki Bhambri kisses the trophy after winning the Boys Singles at the Australian Open tennis championship in Melbourne, Australia.

is now the toast of the nation and the most expensive cricket player in the country. Irfan and Yusuf Pathan, sons of a *maulvi* (religious preacher) are now amongst the richest cricketers of the country and the same story is now repeated with several other players, all of whom have come from backward areas and made a mark in the national and international scene.

A remarkable feature of Indian sports is the spirit of secularism that pervades it. There may have been instances of regionalism but seldom communalism. A few months after Independence, the Indian football team for 1948 London Olympics included four Muslim players — Taj Mohammed, S.M.Kaiser, S.A.Basheer and M.Ahmed Khan — a remarkable feat in itself. At present, the Indian hockey, cricket, football teams comprise a number of players from the minority communities of India.

In the international arena, India has had early, though mixed success. It was an unsung soldier, Kasabha Jadhav who earned India her first individual medal at the 1952 Olympics, the only time the country won two medals in these games, the second occasion being the gold bagged for hockey by a lowly ranked armyman, Dhyan Chand. Tenzing Norgay put the country on the world's sporting map six years after Independence when he, along with Sir Edmund Hillary of New Zealand, became the first man to climb Mount Everest on May 29, 1953. Besides being the undisputed hockey champions, India had also gained international repute in football. It won a gold at the 1951 and '62 Asiad, and made it to the Olympic football semi-finals in Melbourne in 1956. The country produced an individual world champion soon after with Wilson Jones becoming the first Indian to win the World Amateur Billiards Championship in 1958 (he regained the title in 1964 in New Zealand).

At the 1960 Rome Olympics, runner Milkha Singh broke the world record, with a timing of 45.6 seconds in 400 metres, but missed the medal by a whisker. Two other Indian athletes, hurdler Gurbachan Singh Randhawa and middle distance runner Sriram Singh performed creditably in 1964 Tokyo and 1976 Montreal Olympics respectively. Randhawa finished fifth in 110m hurdles in fourteen seconds while Sriram took the seventh place in 800m with a time of 1:45.77 seconds. It remained the Asian record for seventeen years and is still a national record. Shooter Karni Singh stood like a

India's champion woman boxer Mary Kom delivers a punch
at the 4th Asian Women's Boxing Championship in Guwahati.

colossus on the range winning four gold medals at the Oslo World Shooting Championship in 1961.

Tennis star Ramanathan Krishnan twice made it to the semi-finals of Wimbledon Championship 1960 and 1961, losing to eventual champions Neale Fraser and Rod Laver respectively. Krishnan's legacy was nurtured and taken ahead by Vijay Amritraj, who won the first major title for India when he claimed the Volvo Grand Prix at Bretton Woods, USA, in 1973. In the Davis Cup, India thrice reached the

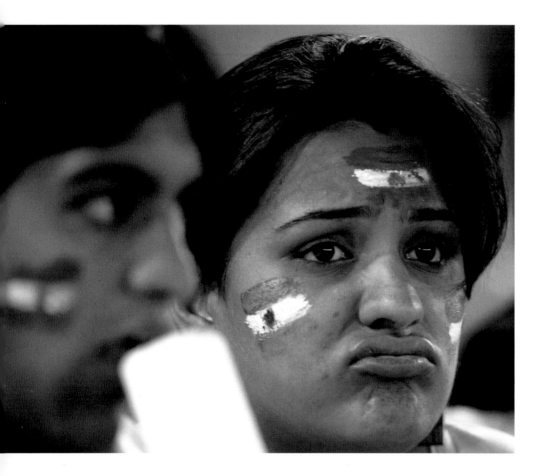

final but lost to Australia (1966) and to Sweden (1987). If Tenzing Norgay touched the skies, Mihir Kumar Sen from Bengal was the first Indian to cross the English Channel in 1958 and was the first Asian to cross the Straits of Gibraltar, between Spain and Tangier. P.G. "Biloo" Sethi, created history when he became the first Indian

amateur to win the Indian Open Golf Championship in 1965 at Delhi. Hockey team which won five gold, a silver and two bronze medals in Olympic Games also claimed the World Cup as the Ajit Pal Singh-led side pipped Pakistan to the post with a 2-1 victory in the final in Kuala Lumpur in 1975.

The above mentioned landmarks demonstrate that Indian sports, despite financial constraints, a lack of infrastructure and minimal government support, did have successes that merited international recognition.

The late 1970s – early 1980s saw the emergence of young Indian world beaters like badminton star Prakash Padukone, tennis players Vijay Amritraj, Ramesh Krishnan and cue players Michael Joseph Ferreira and Geet Sethi. Prakash Padukone became the first Indian to win the All-England Championship, beating Indonesia's Liem Swie King in the final in London in 1980. He also won the first ever World Cup in 1981. Pullela Gopi Chand became the second such player when he won the 2001 All England title. At the 1984 Los Angeles Olympics, P.T. Usha became the first Indian woman to enter the final of an athletics event but missed the 400m hurdles bronze by 1/100th of a second. She finished fourth in 55.42 seconds.

It is in cue sports, billiards and snooker that India has produced world beaters in Michael Joseph Ferreira, Geet Sethi, O.B. Agarwal and Pankaj Advani. Ferreira won the World Amateur and Professional Billiards Championships in 1977. He reclaimed the amateur title in 1981 and 1983. Geet Sethi won the IBSF (International Billiards and Snooker Federation) World Billiards Championship in 1985, 1987 and 2001. He also won the World Professional Billiards titles in 1992, 1993, 1995, 1998 and 2006. In 1984, O.B. Agarwal earned the distinction of being the first Indian to win the World Snooker Championship in Dublin. Teenager Pankaj Advani created history by winning the World Snooker Championship in Beijing in 2003. In 2005, he won the IBSF World Billiards Championship time format and the 150-up format, in Malta.

Indians' passion for cricket is best illustrated in how it rushes them to be upset (*left*) or jubilant (*facing page*) with their team's loss or victory.

Indian golfer Jeev Milkha Singh practises his strokes at the
Augusta National Golf Club in Augusta, Georgia.

(*facing page*) India's rising tennis star Somdev Devvarman in
ATP Chennai Open Tennis tournament in Chennai.

But all these achievements paled into insignificance, with the world cup cricket victory in 1983 and after that, it is cricket and only cricket that has captured imagination. Beating all odds Kapil Dev led India to a stunning win over West Indies by forty-three runs to clinch their only World Cup so far. India also reached the final in 2003, but lost to Australia in Johannesburg. In 1985, Sunil Gavaskar led India to beat Pakistan and clinch the World Championship of Cricket. Gavaskar also, became the first batsman in the world to score 10,000 runs in Test cricket in 1987.

Anil Kumble became the second bowler, after England's Jim Laker, to claim all ten wickets in an innings (10/74) against Pakistan at Delhi in 1999. India won the Under-19 World Cup triumph title in 2000 in Colombo and in 2007 it won the inaugural T20 title. Team India also gained the top slot in 2009 in the ICC world rankings for Test cricket.

In women's cricket, Mithali Raj set the world record as she scored 214 in the third test against England in Taunton in 2002. But cricket was revolutionised when BCCI created a multimillion dollar IPL and it is said cricket will never be the same again.

Despite cricket mania that has swept the country, there are individuals who made Indians proud with their world class performances. Viswanathan Anand is the first Indian to become the world chess champion. He first won the title in 2000. Koneru Humpy became the first Indian girl to win the World Junior Girls Chess Championship in 2001. In shooting, Jaspal Rana won the gold in the junior standard pistol category at the 1994 World Championship. Anjali Bhagwat won the gold in the women's air rifle of the 2003 World Cup. Abhinav Bindra won the 10m air rifle gold medal with 699.1 points (597+102.1) at the 2006 World Championship in Zagreb and then went on to win gold at the

India's ace woman shuttler Saina Nehwal returns
a shot during the 2008 Olympics in Beijing.

India's captain Baichung Bhutia (left) tries to control the ball as Syria's Khaled
M Albaba reacts in the final of the Nehru Cup soccer tournament in New Delhi.
India defeated Syria 1-0 to win the cup.

2008 Beijing Olympics. The Naga girl, Mary Kom created history in boxing with a golden hat trick at the World Championships, winning the 46kg title in Turkey in 2004, in Russia in 2005 and in Delhi in 2006. Prem Chand Degra bagged the Mr Universe title in the middleweight class in Brisbane in 1988. Anthony Maria Irudayam won the singles, doubles (with R. Arokiaraj) and the team titles at the first world carom championship. Weightlifter Kunjarani Devi won India's first gold (in 48kg category) at the Commonwealth Championships in Nauru in 1995, and became the world number one. Archer Jayanta Talukdar won the recurve gold at the 2006 World Cup in Croatia, while Dola Banerjee also bagged the recurve gold at the 2007 World Cup in England.

Arjun Atwal became the first Indian to play in the Professional Golfers Association (PGA) Tour in 2003. He also became the first player on the Asian PGA to overtake USD 1 million in career earnings the same year by winning the USD 300,000 Hero Honda Masters. Jeev Milkha Singh was the first Indian to break into the top fifty of the official world golf rankings last year. Jyoti Randhawa, Shiv Kapur, Gaurav Ghei, Rahil Ganjee are among the numerous other Indian golf stars who are creating waves on the greens all over the world.

There has also been modest success in tennis. In 1996, at the Atlanta Olympics, Leander Paes beat Fernando Meligeni of Brazil to become second Indian to win the Olympic bronze medal. Paes-Bhupathi became the most successful Indian men's pair and won many doubles titles, both at Grand Slam events and on the ATP circuit, as also the Asian Games gold medal in 2002 in Busan and in Doha in 2006. In 2003, Sania Mirza with Russian Alisa Kleybanova, became the first and the youngest Indian woman to win a Grand Slam event when she clinched the junior Wimbledon doubles. She is the first Indian to enter the third round (Australian Open 2005) and the fourth round (US Open 2005) of a senior Grand Slam event. In weightlifting, Karnam Malleswari became the first Indian woman to win an Olympic medal in 2000 when she won the bronze in the 69 kg category lifting 240kg (110kg in snatch and 130kg in clean and jerk).

In long jump, Anju Bobby George cleared 6.70m to win the long jump bronze at the 2003 Paris World Championship. It was the first medal won by an Indian at a global athletics competition.

Rajyavardhan Singh Rathore shot 179 points (135+44) to become the first individual Indian to win the silver medal at the 2004 Athens Olympics.

While India's sports performance has had a chequered history, with both successes and failures, some of the failures deserve special mention. In 2006, India finished tenth in the twelve nation world cup hockey. Same year in the Asian Games for the first time India failed to win a medal in hockey by finishing fifth. This was particularly distressing since India was, at one time, world champions in hockey. Last year, for the very first time, India failed to qualify for the main league format of the World Cricket Cup as they lost, first to Bangladesh and then to Sri Lanka and thus, were eliminated from the cup. The biggest shock for hockey lovers came earlier in 2008 when, for the first time, India failed to qualify for the Olympic hockey competition! In 2008 itself, Indian football sank to a new low, losing to Maldives in SAFF (South Asian Football Federation) final.

Indian Olympic Association (IOA), the supreme sports body in the country, is hopeful that the standard of sports in the country has the potential to improve and that the country could indeed emerge as a leading medal contender in the world arena in coming years. "We have enormous potential, but we have not always tapped it properly," asserted Randhir Singh, secretary general of the Indian Olympic Association (IOA). "Our emphasis has not been on sports; our emphasis has been on water and roads. But economically, India is doing a lot better, and we have the surplus money now…Everyone is waking up," Randhir Singh said, "The economic growth of India is changing the thinking." He is of the view that the government is now keener to develop sports and that with the help of government, the IOA has plans to establish 800,000 sports clubs in villages throughout the country and to build a 150-acre national Olympic training centre. The goal is to "put India on the medals grid" in the 2010 Commonwealth and 2012 Olympics by identifying India's best

Team India celebrates on Marine Drive, Mumbai after winning
the T20 Cricket World cup in 2007.

India's grand master Viswanathan Anand (left) at the
World Chess Championship in Mexico City.

Shooter Abhinav Bindra with his teammate
Gagan Narang sharing a lighter moment.

young athletes and providing them with the resources for training under the best coaches and competing internationally.

However, this is not going to be an easy journey and if there are high expectations from Indian sportspersons, they need to be backed through institutional support.Furthermore, while not detracting from the passion that Indians feel towards cricket, there is need to encourage other sports including those in which India was once known as world beaters. This is easier said than done for it is a fact that Sachin Tendulkar, Rahul Dravid, Sourav Ganguly, Harbhajan Singh, Anil Kumble, Dhoni and many other cricket players are the icons for today's youth. Gavaskar, Tendulkar and Kapil Dev have set world records at various times and the role they have played deserves respect. But to put cricket above all other sports, seems more than a trifle unfair given the fact that cricket is played seriously only in about eight or nine nations in the world.

Yes, it has been a long time since India won a gold medal in Olympic hockey or a title at the All-England Badminton Championships and these, indeed, are sports that India has been steadily making a mark in. Who knows, perhaps the gold medal and the two bronze medals at the Beijing Olympics will set the ball rolling for a turnaround in our attitude towards sports. Perhaps, the Commonwealth Games and the next Olympics will see India fight her way up on the medals table. It can only happen, if all forms of sports become a national passion. Like cricket.

Harpal Singh Bedi is Editor Sports, United News of India. He has been covering sports for the last three decades, including six Olympics, six Asian Games, five cricket world cups and three hockey world cups, besides numerous international and national events and meets.

Shooters Anjula Jung and Anjali Bhagwat smile bright after clinching
the medal for India.

The Indian Polity

Rohan Mukherjee

Winston Churchill once famously proclaimed, "India is a geographical term. It is no more a united nation than the Equator." This succinct observation from the acerbic British Prime Minister encapsulates the paradox of Indian polity. Churchill laid out the challenge, and India's first Prime Minister Pandit Jawaharlal Nehru provided the response, "India is a geographical and economic entity, a cultural unity amidst diversity, a bundle of contradictions held together by strong but invisible threads." Today history sides with Nehru as India strides proudly into its seventh decade of Independence, more contradictory yet more united than ever before. That India is diverse, is now a commonly accepted cliché. In terms of geography, topography, climate, ethnicity, religion, language, culture, income, even caste, India presents a splendid panoply of contradictions. Yet differences that might have fractured most other polities have somehow been accommodated in the Indian case. Who would have thought, at the threshold of Independence in 1947, that India would one day be among the most economically dynamic and politically stable countries of the post-colonial world? This outcome was but a chimera at the time, an almost unattainable goal sought for by a handful of visionary freedom fighters and national leaders. Arising from the throes of a bloody subcontinental partition, and shrugging off over a century and a half of colonial subjugation, India's hesitant steps on the path of sovereignty soon gained confidence as a nation was born, a state formed, a people rejuvenated and the spirit of democracy awakened.

Nowhere is the spark of this spirit stronger than in the Indian Constitution, the crucible of India's heterogeneity, a testament to its collective will to stay united, and a solemn reminder of the principles for which many men and women laid down their lives in the face of external oppression. The very preamble of the Constitution asserts that India is a "sovereign, democratic, republic" — a firm statement that the people of India will be the sole adjudicators of their fate. To this were added the words "socialist" and "secular" in 1976, reaffirming a tacit principle of

India's first Prime Minister Jawaharlal Nehru looks down at the crowd during India's first Independence Day celebrations at Red Fort, New Delhi.

Indian governance that puts the onus of growth and development on the state and requires it to treat all citizens equally. Even in the darkest hours of the intra-communal religious tensions that cast their shadow on the Indian polity from time to time, the Constitution has helped its guardians maintain order, deliver justice and mend temporary ruptures in the sociopolitical fabric. The rule of law treats all individuals as equal while guaranteeing them fundamental rights. The Constitution acts as the cornerstone of Indian polity, which was founded on the ideals of justice, liberty, equality and fraternity.

Government

An exemplary Constitution does not by any means guarantee an impeccable political system. India's polity bears the scars and blemishes of numerous occasions on which the political principles underlying the Constitution have been ignored, abused, or subverted. Moreover, India's territorial and social diversity has placed considerable demands on its polity, pulling it in numerous different directions. Yet the centre does hold, things do not fall apart. The core of Indian democracy retains its vitality and is in fact enriched and deepened each time it is challenged. Part of the credit for this

goes to the way India's government is structured. The exigencies of accommodating divergent social interests and regional differences led the country's founding fathers to opt for a parliamentary democracy with a federal structure. This has created two distinct levels of government that allow for the representation of both local and national interests in the Indian polity.

The pre-eminent lawmaking authority in the country is the Parliament, a highly revered institution that derives its legitimacy and authority from being the only national institution directly representing the people. Specifically, it is the Lok Sabha (the house of the people), the Lower House, which is directly elected by the people. The Rajya Sabha (the council of states), the Upper House, is elected by state legislatures and is thus indirectly elected by the people. The 545 legislators of the Lok Sabha and the 250 legislators of the Rajya Sabha together represent over 1.2 billion individuals — by all means an almost superhuman task. In terms of more local representation, India is divided into thirty states and five federally administered territories. The highest lawmaking authority in a state is the State Legislative Assembly or Vidhan Sabha. This is normally the only house of a state legislature. A small number of states have two houses,

in which case the Vidhan Sabha is the Lower House and the Vidhan Parishad (State Legislative Council) the Upper House.

While the Parliament is the national legislature of India, the national executive is comprised of the President of India and the Council of Ministers (also known as the Cabinet) led by the Prime Minister. The political party that wins the majority of seats in elections to the Lok Sabha forms the government. The Prime Minister comes from this party and is the chief executive of the government. He selects a Cabinet of Ministers to be the inner circle of the government, each of who is in charge of a particular portfolio, e.g. finance, defence, commerce, etc. While the Prime Minister is the head of government, the President of India is the head of state. At state level, the corresponding figures are the Chief Minister and Governor. The President is often described as a nominal head of state, yet he has some important powers that can be brought to bear on the government of the day to influence the formulation of policies but not their outcomes.

Since the late 1980s, no single political party has gained a complete majority in the Lok Sabha. India is now living through an era of coalition governments where different political parties come together to form the government. The resulting governments often lack cohesion and are comprised of opportunistic political elements that tend to reduce politics to the trading of seats and portfolios. Depending on how optimistic one is about Indian democracy, the present could be viewed as its deepening, or the age of policy paralysis. Whatever the analysis, the structure of India's government depicts a finely balanced system that is designed to accommodate the plurality of the Indian situation. The vibrancy of Indian democracy is evident from the frequency with which the predictions of political pundits are confounded by the will of the people, be it in the survival of the Narasimha Rao government of 1991–1996, the ascendancy of the BJP in 1998 and its dramatic loss six years later, or even the re-election of Narendra Modi following the Gujarat riots of 2002. For better or worse, by exercising their right to be represented, Indian people have shown time and again that there is no determinacy to Indian politics, that no government should feel too comfortable in

office unless it can deliver the mandate on which it was elected. This, above all is a sign of a lively and hotly contested political arena.

Parliament

Laws are the backbone of a political system. They set the rules of the game and allow for peaceful resolution of disputes between citizens. The Parliament is the primary lawmaking authority at the national level in India. The gravity of its responsibility can scarcely be understated. Over the years it has built up for itself a

considerable reputation as a responsible and representative body, having earned the trust of millions of Indians who elect the representatives that constitute it. The Parliament is also a vital space for national debates on critical issues impacting the Indian polity. Ever since the days of Pandit Nehru when legislative debating was considered a form of art, and in reality it did approximate this ideal, parliamentarians have considered it their duty to articulate the

Mahatma Gandhi at a 1946 mass meeting in Madras (now Chennai).

(*above*) A symbol of thriving Indian democracy. School children holding the Indian tricolour.

(*Pages 137 – 138*) Bodyguards of the President in the forecourt of Rashtrapati Bhawan in New Delhi.

interests of their constituencies and of the nation in an open forum where ideas can be exchanged in the true spirit of democracy. No doubt talking about issues helps to clarify them and sharpen their relevance to India's national interest, yet they also serve to make Parliament more transparent and legitimate in the eyes of the public.

The importance of Parliament as a legislative body need not be reiterated. However, the complexity of its task requires some attention. The Parliament functions in three sessions during a calendar year — the budget session (February to May), the monsoon session (July to September) and the winter session (November and December). During these sessions the Parliament carries out its various functions, the most important ones being lawmaking and ensuring the accountability of the government and federal bureaucracy. The making of a law is necessarily a long and complicated process. The typical course of an ordinary bill is as

follows: the government identifies the need for a law/amendment in a particular area; it consults widely within its relevant ministries, the state governments, legal experts, interest groups and civil society at large; a proposal finalised in this manner is submitted to the Cabinet for approval; upon approval, the proposal is drafted into a bill and subsequently introduced in Parliament by a member. In the originating house, the bill goes through three stages of reading where it is introduced, studied in detail, then referred to committee and amended if necessary, before being voted on by the entire house.

A bill passed in this manner then goes to the other house, which follows the same stages of reading. This house may accept the bill as it is, it may also make amendments and send the bill back to the originating house, or it may reject the bill. On the rare occasion of a serious disagreement between the two houses,

the President convenes a joint sitting of the two houses presided by the Speaker of the Lok Sabha. In any event, if both houses pass a bill it is sent to the President for his assent. The President can technically withhold his assent, but in practice if he disagrees with a bill then it is sent back to Parliament for clarification or reconsideration. If both houses pass the bill again, the President is left with no choice but to give his assent to the bill, which is then enacted into law. Thus lawmaking emerges as a complex process that has to balance multiple interests and concerns at every stage, making it virtually impossible for the dominance of any particular opinion or ideology over others. This again is a vital sign of democratic health in the Indian polity.

Federalism and Decentralisation

It is commonly said that in India one can encounter a different dialect by travelling twenty-five miles in any direction. Regional diversity is thus a fact of Indian political life. With twenty-nine territorially distinct languages, each spoken by more than one million people, and a multitude of smaller language and dialect groups, communication — the very foundation of civic life — is a complicated matter in India. Moreover, ethnic identities and regional affiliations make national policymaking an incredibly difficult task. This is why federalism presents itself as the most appropriate organising principle of the Indian polity. In essence it means that the various regional communities of India — Tamils, Punjabis, Bengalis, Assamese, Gujaratis, Marathis and others — can exercise some degree of autonomy within their states. The federal government retains exclusive authority in matters of defence, strategic industries, foreign affairs, railways, aviation, mass communication, intellectual property rights, standards in higher education, non-agricultural income tax, corporation tax, etc. while state governments have exclusive authority

in matters of policing, local government, public health, agriculture, water, land, agricultural income tax, etc. Both levels of government have joint authority over criminal law, forests, economic and social planning, employment and social security, education, price control, electricity, etc.

Although the federal government tends to be the more dominant authority in Indian polity, the existence of state governments and federalist principles ensures that regional concerns do not spill over into national conflicts, and that the diverse needs of different communities are given adequate and appropriate representation in governance. A third level of government also exists and has been empowered since the early 1990s to provide for representation at a level even closer to the people than state governments. This has been the result of two constitutional amendments that enhanced and empowered traditional local government institutions (called Panchayati Raj) to become independently elected bodies, one-third of whose composition is set aside for women, with greater powers for planning local economic development and co-ordinating the provision of local services. The Indian polity is therefore complex not just horizontally but also vertically, an inevitable result of a large electorate with diverse needs.

Political Parties

Alexis de Tocqueville once said about American politics that there are many men of principle, but there is no party of principle. The era of coalition governments has ushered in political practices that are all too frequently described by the Indian media as "horse-trading." Opportunism abounds and quid pro quo is the order of the day. Yet elections take place in a relatively free atmosphere and the change of power is relatively frequent and uneventful. Political parties, warts and all, are still the centrepieces of political life in India. They are the chief vehicles by which citizens and their interests are connected and conveyed to the corridors of power. Starting out from a system of one-party dominance in the first two decades of Independence, India today has numerous political parties of varying ideologies and policy agendas.

India is also living in an age of "identity politics" where individual or group identity is equated with interest in the political sphere. Lacking any other avenues for their development, previously excluded and disadvantaged groups like lower castes, religious minorities, or neglected regions have begun to view politics as a means of achieving socioeconomic or other objectives. The result has been a proliferation of small but significant political parties with narrow identity-based electorates that are numerically enough to get them a moderately sized foothold in the Lok Sabha. For instance, the share of seats for state-based parties has more than quadrupled since the first Lok Sabha elections of 1952. In effect it is now much harder for any single party to secure a majority in Parliament. In the period from 1989 to 1998, India witnessed seven successive coalition governments. Under ordinary majority party rule, there should have been at most three governments during this period. While this certainly signifies a more inclusive form of democracy taking root in India, it does not always bode well for the policymaking process, which can be severely crippled by internal political differences in a ruling alliance.

Elections

The most overt symbol of democracy, elections are often described as one of the great festivals of India. Street corners, bazaars, public parks, stadiums — all are commandeered in the campaign effort and adorned with flyers, posters and banners of all colours and shapes, with various political symbols and larger-than-life personalities taking up as much space as policy proposals or election slogans. Large sums of money and considerable human resources are poured into campaigns that span cities, districts, states, and even the country, depending on the type of election. Indeed given the multiplicity of federal, state and local governments, every year witnesses numerous elections that involve hectic activity on the part of political parties, the government, election candidates and, to some extent, the electorate.

Ultimately every citizen's vote is treated equally. This means that a fisherman from coastal Kerala has an equal right to political

The supporters of a political leader sing folk songs during an election rally in Jammu and Kashmir.

representation as a goatherd from the Kashmir valley and a tribal farmer from the hills of Assam. It also means that organising and administering elections is a mammoth task. Come election time, no matter the weather or the terrain, election officials must go out and collect and count every single vote. The conduct of elections is the responsibility of a constitutional body called the Election Commission of India. The sheer scale of activity undertaken by the Commission is evident from the recent 2009 Lok Sabha elections, which saw almost 417 million voters (a turnout of 58 per cent)

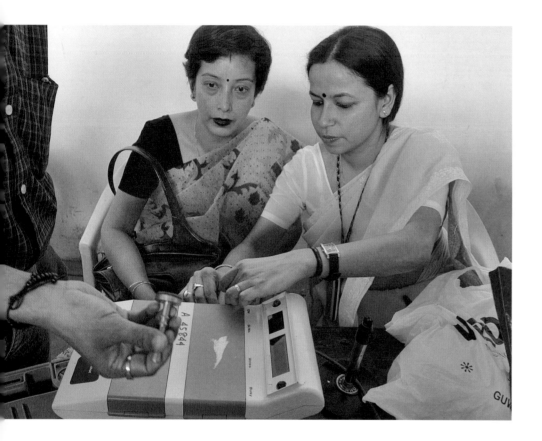

casting their ballot at 8,20,000 polling stations located in widely varying geographical conditions. The election was contested by 370 political parties with an average of fourteen candidates competing in a constituency. In order to ensure the smooth running of the election, the Commission employed close to 6.1 million civil and security personnel. The total cost of the election was approximately USD 268 million.

Judiciary and Civil Society

Elections are important, but a vote cast once every five years cannot and does not significantly influence government policies in the intervening period. Nor can it ensure that government actions during this period do not infringe the rights of citizens or indirectly harm them in any way. To understand accountability in the Indian polity, one therefore turns to the judiciary and civil society. India's judiciary is a highly respected institution that is widely regarded as the guardian of the Constitution. Extending in a hierarchy from the Supreme Court down to High Courts at state level and District Courts and numerous civil and criminal courts, the judiciary has over time become entrenched as the guardian of civil liberties and adjudicator of disputes in Indian society. Civil society, the second pillar of accountability, is comprised of diverse organisations including the media, interest groups, non-governmental organisations (NGOs) and professional associations. The Right to Information campaign, spearheaded by civil society, succeeded in bringing about national level legislation that made government agencies more transparent. Through innovative programming, new channels of communication and by involving citizens in the reporting and analysis of public events, television channels, radio stations and newspapers have broken new ground in bringing government closer to the governed. A simple example in this regard has been the launch of the 'Lok Sabha' television channel that provides a window into the inner world of Parliament.

Conclusion

India represents a fascinating mosaic of diversity in almost every possible aspect of its national life. A glimpse at the manner in which its polity has managed this diversity in order to become a successful and vibrant democracy is highlighted here. The project is by no means complete, yet strong institutions have taken hold and provide us with much hope for the future. To complete Pandit Nehru's thoughts on India, "She is a myth and an idea, a dream and a vision, and yet very real and present and pervasive." Despite its complexities, drawbacks and inadequacies, India's democratic experiment is firmly underway and set to capture the imagination of the world for years to come.

Election officials check an electronic voting machine in Guwahati.

(*facing page*) Indian election officials carry electronic voting machines and other election material atop elephants to the remote village of Barkhashung in Dispur constituency, Assam.

The Election Commission of India

Elections are a vital ingredient of Indian democracy since they determine the extent to which various competing groups in society are represented politically. The sheer size and diversity of the country make elections a complex and intricate affair, requiring the highest order of organisational management. Moreover, given the high stakes involved, it is critical that elections are managed smoothly, efficiently, transparently and authoritatively. Fortunately, the Election Commission of India has proved itself capable of doing all this and more.

Established in 1950, the Commission is a constitutional body responsible for the superintendence, direction and control of all elections to federal and state legislatures, as well as elections to the office of the President and Vice-President. It consists of three members — two Election Commissioners and one Chief Election Commissioner (CEC) who make decisions by majority vote. They are appointed by the President for terms of six years and have the same status as judges of the Supreme Court of India. The CEC can only be removed from his position through impeachment by the Parliament.

For its day-to-day functioning, the Commission relies on a secretariat of approximately 300 officials with an independent budget. These officials are organised into functional divisions like planning, judicial administration, information systems, media and secretariat coordination, as well as territorial divisions based on geographical zones. The importance of order and hierarchy for effective management of elections is apparent in the functioning of the secretariat, and the functioning of the ECI in the states. Each state is supervised by a Chief Electoral Officer, each district by a District Election Officer, and each federal or state constituency has a Returning Officer responsible for conducting elections and an Electoral Registration Officer responsible for preparing and maintaining electoral rolls. Each polling station is supervised by a Presiding Officer and manned by Polling Officers. In addition, the Commission appoints Observers in each constituency to ensure fairness and transparency of elections. Aside from the secretariat and state level electoral officials, the rest of the officials in this hierarchy are not permanent but are officials from other departments and agencies deputed for election purposes.

The defining characteristic of the Commission is its independence from other organs of government and political parties. It is insulated from executive interference and even the judiciary cannot question the Commission functioning unless a specific petition on the matter is filed in a High Court or the Supreme Court. In order to contest elections, political parties must register with the ECI, which grants recognition based on whether a party is internally democratic and committed to the principles enshrined in the Indian Constitution. The Commission also enforces a rigorous 'Model Code of Conduct' during elections that regulates the behaviour of candidates and parties to ensure a level playing field.

Over the years, the Commission has taken many innovative steps to fulfil its constitutional mandate, including an active media campaign to promote political awareness among voters, the computerisation of electoral rolls, issuing photo identity cards for voters and introducing Electronic Voting Machines (EVMs). In sum, the ECI has emerged as a highly respected institution in the Indian polity and a symbol of democratic stability and dynamism. For more information visit the website of the Election Commission of India at www.eci.gov.in.

Rohan Mukherjee is a student of public affairs at the Woodrow Wilson School, Princeton University. His academic interests are in international affairs and the political economy of development. His professional life has taken him from the tribal belt of northern Orissa to the policy making circles in New Delhi. He is still learning the intricacies of everything in between.

A security person keeps vigil atop the state legislature building during the swearing-in ceremony of a chief minister in Bangaluru.

(*Pages 145 – 146*) Over the years, white Ambassador cars with red beacons have denoted the power of Executive in India. A fleat of them in the backdrop of Rashtrapati Bhawan, New Delhi.

India's Economic Tryst with Destiny

Bibek Debroy

"Long years ago we made a tryst with destiny, and now the time comes when we shall redeem our pledge, not wholly or in full measure, but very substantially. At the stroke of the midnight hour, when the world sleeps, India will awake to life and freedom." No Indian need be told this is Jawaharlal Nehru's 'tryst with destiny' speech, delivered on the midnight of 14/15 August 1947.

It didn't quite work that way and India didn't redeem the economic pledge. Per capita income is an average indicator of how rich or how poor a country's citizens are. Depending on the source (World Bank, IMF) and the year (in cross-country comparisons, there is a time lag of about two years on data), India's per capita income is now around USD 1017. The richest country in the world (Luxembourg) has a per capita income of around USD 113,044. A rank of 143 out of 180 countries isn't particularly comforting. True, this USD 1017 is based on official exchange rates, such as Rs 45 to USD 1. And Rs 45 can buy more in India than USD 1 can in the US. This takes one to the notion of Purchasing Power Parity (PPP). India's PPP per capita income of USD 2,780 looks a bit more respectable. However, our rank is still 130. The euphoria about India usually concerns the size of the economy. For instance, using official exchange rates and with European Union not being counted as a single entity, the Indian economy is twelfth largest in the world. If one uses PPP instead, the Indian economy is fourth largest in the world, after US, China and Japan. The euphoria is also not about what the state is today, but about what is likely to happen in the future. By 2025, the Indian economy will be the third largest in the world (after US and China), regardless of whether one uses PPP or not. But this large income is also distributed over a large population of 1.20 billion.

A worker near the Mumbai International Airport.

India still remains a poor country. Depending on which figure one uses, 28 per cent of the population is still below the poverty line and 27.5 per cent of the Indian population is more than the populations of most countries of the world. The life expectancy at birth is only 63.8 years. 47 per cent of children under the age of five are underweight. The adult literacy rate (for those older than fifteen) is only 61 per cent. Per capita income doesn't capture everything about poverty. Since 1990, United Nations Development Programme (UNDP) has brought out a Human Development Report (HDR) and this computes a Human Development Index (HDI) based on PPP per capita income, education (literacy, gross enrollment ratio) and health (life expectancy). According to HDI, India has a rank of 134 out of 182 countries. The promised tryst with destiny should have been better.

India has had five year plans since 1951. One way to track what has happened to the economy since Independence is to look at real rates of Gross Domestic Product (GDP) growth across these plans. For the First Plan (1951 – 56), the annual average real growth was 4.4 per cent. It was 3.8 per cent for the Second Plan (1956 – 61) and 2.6 per cent for the Third Plan (1961 – 66). There was a break in planning for three years and the Fourth Plan (1969 – 74) produced 3.1 per cent. These kinds of numbers lead to coinage of the expression Hindu rate of growth, because India never seemed to be able to get out of that trend of 3.5 per cent. Per capita growth was lower still. With that kind of growth, one couldn't have hoped to make much dent on poverty and unemployment. India also fell behind in cross country comparisons. Jawaharlal Nehru's imagery was geographically incorrect. When it was midnight in India, the rest of the world wasn't sleeping. It was wide awake. References are often made to miracle growth rates in East Asia, beginning with Japan, then Hong Kong, South Korea, Taiwan and Singapore, then Indonesia, Malaysia and Thailand and finally China. In the very early 1960s, regardless of which development indicator one uses, India performed better than many of these tiger economies. Indeed, in the late 1950s, India was often projected as a role model by many development economists. The 1960s and 1970s were lost development decades, when many other economies outstripped

India. India never seemed to recover from the wars of 1962 and 1965 and droughts in the mid-1960s. Why did this happen? In part, the answer lies in dysfunctional economic policies.

Since Independence, Indian policy was based on planning and a mixed economy, identified as protection, import substitution, the public sector, heavy industry, industrial licensing and extensive government controls. These days, it is easy to denigrate everything that happened since Independence. And it is also fashionable to argue everything changed with reforms in 1991, as if one was writing on a clean slate. For three reasons, one should be careful. First, the worst excesses of government intervention didn't occur in 1950s or early 1960s. That happened from the mid-1960s to late 1970s. Second, had it not been for the policies of 1950s and early 1960s, several phenomena India is proud of (broad and diversified industrial base, strengths in higher education, science and technology, even the Green Revolution of late 1960s) wouldn't have occurred. The problem was in continuing and even intensifying, outdated policies when their costs were turning out to be more than their benefits. India ought to have opened up in late 1960s. Third, there was some limited attempt at opening up in late 1970s and 1980s, though this wasn't as systematic and comprehensive as what has happened since 1991. The Fifth Plan (1974 – 79) produced average annual GDP growth of 4.9 per cent. After a break in planning for a year, the Sixth Plan (1980 – 85) produced 5.4 per cent and the Seventh Plan (1985 – 90) produced 5.5 per cent. This was a clear break from the trend of 3.5 per cent. Growth had been jacked up to around 5.5 per cent. Those who believed in reforms legitimately argued that if limited reforms could produce this, imagine what more systematic reforms would accomplish.

The present reforms date to 1991 and were unilateral. They weren't thrust down Indian throats by World Bank or IMF as the sceptics would like us to believe. Ever since late 1970s, some economists and a succession of government committee reports had argued in favour of opening up. The diagnosis is simple. Poverty alleviation requires growth. Growth requires efficiency. Efficiency requires competition. That's been the lesson elsewhere in the world.

A woman at work in the paddy fields of Palakad, Kerala.

Why should India be different? The argument that there has been no debate about reforms in India is non sequitur. Didn't these government committee reports represent a debate? However, policy didn't change, because there was no crisis. That crisis came in the form of an external sector Balance Of Payments (BOP) problem in 1990 – 91, triggered partly by the Gulf War. The reasons don't matter any more. Because of this crisis, India unilaterally reformed, before going to IMF for aid. In that legal kind of sense, India didn't reform because of IMF (or World Bank) conditionalities. Those were pre-empted.

What were these reforms? Since reforms were triggered by an external sector crisis, most of these initial reforms concerned the external sector — reduction in tariffs, elimination of quantitative restrictions on imports and exports, rationalisation of export incentives, a realistic market-determined exchange rate of the rupee (with transition towards convertibility), an open policy on Foreign Direct Investments (FDI) and foreign institutional investments.

Most successes ascribed to reforms are also external in nature (such as export growth, improvement in debt indicators, capital inflows, size of foreign exchange reserves, pressures on rupee appreciation). Export growth has averaged 20 per cent and more in US dollar terms for several years. If openness is defined as share of exports and imports in GDP, most people don't know India is today more open than the US. Nor do most people know that since 1990s, India is no longer a net foreign aid recipient. It is a net foreign aid giver (including to IMF) and offers aid to twenty-three countries. There is an excess of foreign exchange reserves. Since these have to be invested in safe assets that fetch a very low rate of return, a debate rages in India about how one can best make use of these excess reserves. Before 1991, average annual FDI inflows into India used to be between 150 and USD 200 million. Tentative figures are that FDI inflow was USD 35.2 billion in 2008 – 09. The bulk of FDI comes from Mauritius and Singapore (because of a tax avoidance treaties), US, UK and Netherlands, in that order. Again, several people don't know that FDI out of India is also significant now, with a figure of USD 15 billion in 2007 – 08, though methods for measuring FDI out of India are not as good as those for measuring FDI into India. A large chunk of this is mergers and acquisitions. Many large Indian companies, particularly in manufacturing, went through a shakeout towards the end of the 1990s, forced by competition. They are leaner and more competitive now. Mergers and acquisitions have been driven by the desire to generate economies of scale and scope as also are a market entry device. However, costs of doing business in India are still too high, documented in World Bank's 'Doing Business' database. These costs also contribute to driving business abroad. On the external sector, India is a capital scarce country in relative terms. Therefore, India should have a current account deficit, though this calculation is complicated by substantial amounts of crude oil India has to import. Yet, from 2001 – 02 to 2003 – 04, India had a current account surplus, explained largely by invisibles or service sector exports.

Although India is relatively more open now, given the large economy the country is, the external sector can only be a small component of the canvas. The hype about IT, software exports, H1B visas, outsourcing and the world turning flat still touches a small

Indian pickles and spices, which are loved for their piquant taste, at a festival in Munich.

Early morning fishing at Cochin. Indian fish has a huge market abroad which means a generous income for the country. Where, on one hand, traditional methods of fishing are being adhered to, encouraged by government aids and policies, on the other, new techniques and machinery is being welcomed.

part of the population. Therefore, after listing the external sector successes, one should focus on what happened to the rest of the economy. The jacking up of growth to a 5.5 per cent trend in 1980s has already been mentioned. After the Seventh Plan, there was a break from planning for two years, coinciding with reforms of 1991 and the immediate effects. Then the Eighth Plan (1992 – 97) produced average annual real growth of 6.7 per cent and the Ninth Plan (1997 – 2002) had 5.3 per cent. The Tenth Plan (2002 – 07) had 7.8 per cent. Till around 2002, growth inched up from 5.5 per cent to around 6.5 per cent. At that time, most forecasters used to project the economy would grow at around this rate. However, what has happened since 2003 – 04 is spectacular. The economy has grown at close to 9 per cent, sometimes exceeding it and future projections focus on how a 9 per cent plus growth rate can be sustained. This means a medium term trend, not the cyclical downturn that is certain for the next few years. With growth touching 9 per cent, more external attention has focused on India and there has been euphoria and bullishness. This is despite the slowdown since 2007-08, impacted partly by the global crisis, National accounts figures suggest the worst of the crisis is now over and in 2009-10, growth should inch back to around 7.5%.

Why has this increase in the growth trajectory to 9 per cent or thereabouts occurred? There are several reasons. First, there has been an unshackling of entrepreneurship, consequent to post-1991 reforms. Second, there has been an increase in the investment rate. Quite often, a contrast used to be drawn between India and China, arguing that Indian growth was consumption-driven, whereas Chinese (and East Asian) growth rates were investment-driven. By implication, one also sometimes tended to argue that high Indian growth rates were unsustainable, because investment rates weren't high enough. However, a convergence seems to be occuring and that dichotomy is somewhat artificial. For example, by 2007 – 08, the Indian savings rate (as share of GDP) increased to 37.7 per cent and the investment rate (foreign savings also contribute to this) increased to 39.1 per cent. So far as household savings are concerned, higher income growth contributed to the increase. But public and corporate savings have also gone up. The simple point is that the savings rate

should increase to 38 per cent and more and investment rate to 40 per cent and more, not that different from East Asian levels. Third, the capital/output ratio is a measure of how efficiently capital is used. At one point, the capital/output ratio used to be as high as 6. Today, it is around 4. Competition has spurred efficiency and reductions in the capital/output ratio. More importantly, there has been a sectoral shift. For instance, the capital/output ratio is 5 in agriculture and allied activities, 8.9 in manufacturing and lower in many services sectors. Because of the structural shift in Indian GDP, more and more of national income originates from services (55 per cent now) and less and less from agriculture and allied activities (around 18 per cent now). Therefore, the overall capital/output ratio drops. Fourth, because of this structural shift, since agriculture and allied activities have performed rather poorly in relative terms, there is automatically a higher rate of GDP growth. Fifth, yet another dichotomy between India and China is often mentioned, to the effect that Indian growth is based on services and Chinese growth is based on manufacturing. There are several question marks about such generalisations. A lot of what is classified as services in India is classified as manufacturing in China. That apart, Indian manufacturing growth has suffered in the last few months because of interest rate hikes. Before that, Indian manufacturing didn't perform that badly, especially since 2004 – 05. No country has generated 9 per cent plus growth rates based on services alone. That was yet another point mentioned when one argued that high Indian growth rates were unsustainable. But since 2004 – 05 (with slightly lower rates, since 2002 – 03), Indian manufacturing has done much better, high export growth contributing to this.

Sixth, there is the labour input component. The dependency ratio (percentage of population outside working age groups) has dropped and will drop further. This has to be contrasted against aging populations, not just in developed countries, but in China too. At differing levels of economic development, countries compete on the basis of different parameters. At low levels of development, competitiveness is based on natural resources and labour. As one moves up the ladder, one graduates to parameters like efficiency (productivity) and innovation. In the forseeable future, India's

The facade of the Bombay Stock exchange is seen reflected on a car wind screen as people watch a display of the Sensex reaching 20,000 points in Mumbai.

competitiveness will be based on availability of labour, the so-called demographic dividend. India is going through a process of demographic transition that East Asia went through earlier. Companies recognise this. Cross-border movements of labour aren't quite substitutes for off-sourcing, they aren't always in the same segment. However, there is some trade-off. Therefore, if US clamps down on cross-border movements through visa restrictions, US companies will simply move their operations to India. Indeed, that's better for India, because multiplier benefits (taxes, consumption expenditure, indirect income growth and employment) then occur in India rather than in US. Notwithstanding protectionist sentiments, downward pressures on wages and some unemployment, in an overall welfare sense, the tapping of India's labour cost advantage is good for

the US economy too. Did the US economy eventually suffer when blue collar jobs were lost to East Asia? The loss of whitecollar jobs may be more visible and vocal. But the same logic applies here too. The economy simply moves on to higher levels of productivity and innovation.

In the internal Indian debate on reforms, a question is often posed. What has this India Shining story done for the poor? Haven't the growth and prosperity stories been pro-rich and urban-centric? Let's have the facts first. The percentage of population below the poverty line in 2004 – 05 was 27.5 per cent according to one definition of the poverty line and 21.8 per cent according to another definition and rural/urban figures are more or less the same.

These figures are high and declines should have been more. However, from around 1950 to around 1980, the percentage of population below the poverty line was flat at 50 per cent. From 50 per cent to 27.5 per cent or 21.8 per cent is a sharp fall, demonstrating that growth does have an impact on poverty declines. Nor is it the case that inequality is very high in India. It has increased a bit for urban India, but is still lower than most countries in the world and has not increased at all for rural India. The rural/urban distinction and the argument that rural India has suffered while urban India has prospered, will not wash. In parts of India that have grown fast, it is impossible to figure out today where rural ends and urban begins. Arguments based on religion, caste or gender don't quite wash either. With the exception of STs (Scheduled Tribes), who tend to be geographically concentrated, poverty has dropped everywhere. Education (enrollment in schools more than literacy) indicators have also improved, though improvements in health indicators haven't been fast enough. Many of the Millennium Development Goals are centred on health and India's performance there hasn't yet been good enough. Government documents talk about inclusive growth and divides and disparities. The most important divide today is geographical or spatial. There are states where growth and poverty declines haven't been fast enough. Among major states, one would include Madhya Pradesh, Chhattisgarh, Uttar Pradesh, Bihar, Orissa, Jharkhand and some parts of the North-East, a belt extending from central India towards the east. Those are the regions one needs to worry about.

(*Pages 155 – 156*) The Indian automobile industry from being the tenth
largest in the world is fast on its way to become one of the majors.

The effervescent mall culture which entails massive investments
and huge risks seems to be driving the Indian retail industry.

To mainstream prosperity there and sustain 9 per cent plus overall growth, one needs to mention the unfinished agenda of reforms. This has a lot to do with where government intervention is necessary, since markets cannot take care of everything. First, there is an issue of targeting the poor, so they can be subsidised. Identification of Below Poverty Line (BPL) households is still unsatisfactory. Second, there is a law and order cum governance issue, including regulation when entry is opened up to the private sector. As a subset of this, the legal regime needs to improve. Third, rural sector reforms (credit, insurance, extension services, disintermediation of distribution chains, land markets, infrastructure) need to happen, since 72 per cent of the population is still classified as rural. This will enable employment creation outside traditional and unproductive agriculture, where 90 per cent of the 100 million landholdings are suboptimal. Fourth, infrastructure needs to improve and some areas of infrastructure (rural roads, electricity generation, drinking water, irrigation water) can't depend on private sector provisioning. Some areas have shown improvements — not just telecom, but roads too. Infrastructure expenditure as share of GDP has increased from 3.5 per cent to 6.5 per cent, though China's 10 per cent is still far away. The most visible failure is in the area of power. Fifth, social infrastructure also needs improvement and here too, some areas (rural schools, primary health centres) need government provisioning. A demographic dividend can't be tapped if mortality and morbidity levels are high and skills and education lacking. Sixth, the efficiency of public expenditure needs to improve and this too, is part of the governance agenda. Tax and Public Sector Undertakings (PSU) reforms are required to ensure that the government has the revenue to do what it needs to do.

A lot has changed in India since 1991. A lot more will change. To use the cliched expression, the glass can be half-empty or half-full. However, it is filling up and as one looks forward towards 2020, the glass will be three-quarters full.

The Indian Planning Commission

The Planning Commission was set up in 1950. The original focus of the Commission was on efficient allocation of resources through formulation of a plan and its monitoring. However, the focus has changed with liberalisation and reliance on the market and from centralised planning, the country has moved towards indicative planning. But resource allocation of public funds still remains an issue and the Planning Commission has to mediate between the requirements of Central government ministries and states. To make it more specific, the Planning Commission formulates Five Year Plans, Annual Plans and State Plans and then monitors programmes, projects and schemes under the same. The Planning Commission works under the supervision of the National Development Council and the Prime Minister is the Chairman of the Commission. The Deputy Chairman has the rank of a Cabinet Minister and the present Deputy Chairman is Montek Singh Ahluwalia. There are full-time members, though the Commission also seeks expertise from outside. Functionally, the Planning Commission operates through divisions, taskforces and committees and it is a rich source of data and studies. Increasingly its Centre-state role is emerging to be pivotal. The web address is www.planningcommission. nic.in.

Bibek Debroy is professor, International Management Institute; research professor, Centre for Policy Research and senior research fellow, Institute for South Asian Studies, National University of Singapore. An economist, he is the author of several papers, popular articles and books and has been a member of many government appointed task forces, committees and commissions. At present, he is also contributing editor with the *Indian Express* group.

(*Pages 159 – 160*) Tea estates, Munnar — tea is indigenous to India and the industry has held world leadership for over 150 years, accounting to 31 per cent of global production.

The Press in India

Tarun Basu

Sir Harold Evans, the legendary editor of *The Times* and *Sunday Times* of UK, had a remarkable story to tell when he was in India in 2007. He was in charge of the first media workshop organised by the International Press Institute to train Indian journalists at the request of Prime Minister Jawaharlal Nehru, who complained that the Indian press was still stuck in the Victorian mode after Independence.

At one of the workshops, Evans remembers talking about how a good headline consisted of simple words in the active voice, such as in the old definition of what makes news — "Man bites Dog." A journalist immediately got up to inform him angrily, "There has been no reported case of a man biting a dog in independent India." From that time in the 1950s, in the immediate afterglow of Independence when the media remained a vehicle for promotion of nationalist ideas and Western concepts, including those in journalism were considered antithetical, India has grown to be one of the world's most vibrant, diverse, exciting and, as its critics would say, sometimes wanton media.

Go to any marketplace, and you are sure to find the news vendor with his wide and rich array of newspapers and magazines of every genre, description, language and origin — including a clutch of foreign publications — a media bouquet that is almost overflowing with choices for every kind of reader. Go closer, and you can find, especially in the morning, people picking up headlines from their newspapers, animatedly discussing the latest national and global happenings, or leafing through magazines. The newspaper stall becomes, in many ways, an intellectual rendezvous where opinions are exchanged and views traded, reflecting the heterodoxy in the thought processes of this clamorous nation of

Men grasp the news of the day at a busy stretch in Connaught Place, New Delhi.

1.20 billion people in what Nobel Laureate Amartya Sen calls its "argumentative tradition".

Although history records that the first newspaper in India came out in 1780 when an Englishman named James Augustus Hicky printed the weekly *Bengal Gazette*, it hardly marked the advent of Indian journalism as it catered primarily to the colonial elite, its military adventures, its social lifestyle and its quaint experiences with those referred to patronisingly as the "natives". The first daily newspaper, again in Bengal, was called the *Hurkaru* and was brought out in 1819 by an Englishman called James Sutherland. It was the only five-column single-sheet newspaper of its time and the interests and resources of several Calcutta journals were merged into it over a period of time.

The first truly Indian newspaper came out almost forty years later, in 1820, when Raja Rammohun Roy, the social reformer, brought out three newspapers in Bengali, Persian and English to counter the sustained tirade by several British colonial publications against Indian religious and social customs and to educate Indians on the need to bring about social changes. These three newspapers marked the true beginning of Indian journalism and were the first among Indian-owned newspapers that we know were published on a regular basis. When a British government functionary sought to put

curbs on these publications, Roy and media patrons like Dwarkanath Tagore, grandfather of Nobel Laureate Rabindranath Tagore, penned an appeal which said that a free press may never have caused a revolution, but revolutions had been innumerable where no free press existed to ventilate grievances. Protesting the media restrictions, Roy closed down *Mirat ul Akhbar*, the Persian language weekly that gave much space to international affairs and their relevance to the Indian situation.

On the west coast, Fardoonjee Marzban founded a Gujarati daily newspaper, *Mumbai Samachar*, in 1822 and it has the distinction of being the oldest Indian newspaper still being published.

The Indian penchant for free expression has a long intellectual history, particularly in eastern India, giving birth to the post-Independence culture of a free press and its numerous legal championing. Its importance cannot be but overstated given the restrictive environment in which the press operates in most less developed countries.

The post-Independence years were marked by a gradual process of Indianisation of the media with the British proprietors selling their stakes and repatriating their proceeds as they feared

curbs on free media operations by nationalist governments in a newly emerging nation. Bennett, Coleman & Co. sold *The Times of India* to Seth Ramkrishna Dalmia, a leading industrialist with diverse commercial interests. The *Madras Mail* changed hands, as did *The Statesman* of Calcutta.

On the news agency front, Reuters' Indian subsidiary, the Associated Press of India, which incidentally was formed by four intrepid Bengali journalists before it was swallowed up by Reuters, became the forerunner of the present Press Trust of India (PTI), which grew to become India's and one of Asia's largest news agencies.

Though the Indian Constitution does not expressly guarantee freedom of the press, like the First Amendment of the US Constitution has done, the country's rights' vigilant Supreme Court has held in successive judgments that freedom of the press is covered, and is an essential part of freedom of expression guaranteed by Article 19. Nevertheless, except for the Emergency rule of Prime Minister Indira Gandhi (June 1975 – March 1977), when fundamental rights were suspended and the media was put in fetters, the press in India has remained largely free, as compared to other countries in the region and beyond where a state controlled media or a compliant one existed in the name of ensuring social harmony and economic progress.

Today, the Indian press is widely recognised as the most pluralistic, the least inhibited and the most independent in the less developed world. A content revolution began as soon as the Emergency and press censorship ended. With aggressive investigative journalism that delved into the excesses of the Emergency, the newspapers and many newly launched magazines started to assert their role as watchdogs of society looking critically at all sectors of the nation.

The decade of the 1990s can be truly called transformational, for the Indian media saw the convergence of many changes in the country — the liberalisation of the economy, the loosening of many regulations, the advent of satellite television and the improvement in communication technology. In recent years there has been a virtual explosion in the news media. There are more than 50,000 – 60,000 print media news publications and over 200 news and current affairs television channels, with both television and newspapers expected to grow at 14 per cent CAGR (compounded annual growth rate) during 2010-15 and showing no signs of levelling despite the economic slowdown.

The reach of television (there are now nearly 400 registered television channels in the country) has now exceeded that of the print media while the Internet has captured the attention of a growing

urban and aspirational middle class, eager to connect with the world.

The morphing nature of news across media — be it print, TV, online or mobile — changed media habits, opened a new public discourse and became a major influencer of government policy, political thinking, community lifestyles and social mores. Growing literacy and new technology has resulted in India becoming one of the most exciting media markets in the world. Along with China, the two countries account for 45 of the world's 100 newspapers; but India has more daily newspapers than any other country and leads in paid-for daily circulation. And this is in marked contrast to most of the industrialised nations, especially the US, where newspaper circulations have been dipping steadily and many iconic publications have either shut shop or have been downsizing.

With the mobile phone revolution that is currently going on in India, the country already has the world's second largest subscriber base of 500 million behind China, and is adding 12-15 million subscribers every month. That means by 2010 nearly half the country's population would be mobile phone subscribers. This in turn is adding to the burgeoning numbers of news consumers in India as news gets dispersed across different platforms, creating a new breed of readers/viewers who use one or multiple platforms to access information anywhere, anytime who do not just wait for the morning newspaper.

In the battle for time share, Indian consumers are now spending sixty minutes consuming news every day if one averages the total time across newspapers, TV news and online. And in 2007, advertisers spent over Rs 120 billion (USD 3 billion) to reach them in those sixty minutes, according to data put together by Starcom Worldwide. Add in subscription money, news is roughly a Rs 160 billion (USD 4 billion) market. That makes it the second largest media

(*Pages 163 – 164*) A plethora of OB vans signifying the thriving Indian television news channels, outside the Indian Parliament building, New Delhi.

A television camera crew at work as monsoon clouds loom large in the Delhi sky.

business in India after entertainment, in audience share, profits and now investor interest.

According to a report released in December 2009 by the Associated Chambers of Commerce and Industry (Assocham) and consultancy firm PricewaterhouseCoopers, the Indian entertainment and media industry is estimated to grow 11 per cent annually to touch Rs. 93,200 crore (USD 18.6 billion) by 2013.

The television industry will continue to be the major contributor to the overall revenue pie, growing at 15 per cent yearly over the next five years. The print media, despite the economic pressures, would grow by 5.6 per cent yearly over 2009-13, reaching Rs 21,500 crore from the present level of Rs 16,500 crore.

The growth of the Indian media industry is nowhere best reflected than in the stock market where nearly ten media companies are listed, each with a company valuation of over Rs 1,000 crore (Rs 10,000 million/USD 250 million). The current scenario is a far cry from about two decades ago when the largest media company reported net profits of about Rs 5 crores (Rs 50 million/a little over a million dollars). It's a hundred times than that today.

Some of the largest media companies, like Bennett, Coleman & Co. (that publishes *The Times of India* and associated publications) and Kasturi & Co. (publishers of *The Hindu*) are not even listed. If floated on the stock exchange, Bennett, Coleman & Co. could well be worth more than a couple of billion dollars, say media analysts. It is by far India's largest and most profitable media company and its flagship newspaper, *The Times of India* claims to be the world's largest English language daily with a circulation of 2.4 million.

The rapid expansion and diversification of the Indian press, at a time when the Western world is talking about the demise of the newspaper by 2030, is in a large measure due to the country's growing population, accompanied by rising literacy levels, particularly in the hitherto backward Hindi speaking heartland and the explosion of the aspirational class estimated at 42 per cent of the population (between fifteen to thirty-four years) that has ridden on the country's sustained economic growth over the last decade.

The Indian Newspaper Society (INS), an organisation for the print media in India, says it has over 990 dailies, bi-weeklies, weeklies, fortnightlies and monthlies as members. They publish in eighteen languages from all over the country, accounting for over 90 per cent of the national readership.

The largest growth in readership has by far been in the so-called "Hindi belt" in North and Central India. During the last decade of the twentieth century, literacy expanded in what was earlier called the "Bimaru" (acronyms for Bihar, Madhya Pradesh, Rajasthan and Uttar Pradesh, but literally meaning sick states) region, picking up readers from across its myriad villages and small towns dismissed previously as marketing black holes. Newspapers brought increased awareness, a growing consumerism and civic participation.

The rapid spread of television created an awareness and hunger for news. The advent of Internet made possible the transmission of entire newspaper pages to far-flung districts through what were oddly enough called 'modem centres' for printing locally for quick and cheaper circulation. Expanding telecommunications made multi-edition newspapers more viable and affordable.

"The expansion of Hindi newspaper industry has been unimaginable. The Hindi paper is not just sold in the Hindi heartland but in many other regions of India where it is not the first language of communication," says Shashi Shekhar, editor of

Hindustan, the Hindi language newspaper of the Hindustan Times group. For instance, in Punjab, the circulation of Hindi newspapers is more than the sum of Urdu and Punjabi newspapers. Similarly in Jammu and Kashmir, the Hindi newspaper *Amar Ujala* occupies the number one position whereas Urdu and Punjabi are the most spoken languages there.

The growth and spread of Hindi journalism has gone beyond traditional platforms to new frontiers such as television and online journalism. Today there are numerous Hindi news channels and news portals available online. One can find enthusiastic bloggers from faraway and remote places such as Ratlam and Mirzapur. "The press was moving from being elite to a mass medium. And the Indian newspaper was evolving from being a politics-driven product for the serious minded reader into one that was fashioning itself for the upwardly mobile, as well as for the reader who had barely begun to read," wrote media industry analyst Sevanti Ninan in her seminal book, *Headlines from the Heartland* on the phenomenal rise of the Hindi media.

A common sight across India, particularly in the semi-rural and rural areas, is of people sitting on wooden benches or on their haunches over glasses of steaming tea in roadside stalls, called *dhaba*s, and pouring over newspapers. The *dhaba* owner subscribes to these newspapers to attract the morning gentry. In rural areas, these newspapers are often read out to those who are not so literate and, typically, a newspaper sometimes can be read or shared by a few dozen people. In some progressive villages, newspaper pages, or newspaper headlines, are put up or scrawled on village notice boards, serving as a force multiplier for the spread of news and information.

A decade and a half beginning from early 1990s, the expansion and re-invention of the public sphere in the Hindi belt made the media business both inclusive and more commercially driven. Print went from being elite to mass medium and very ordinary people living in very small towns and villages became both news consumers and newsmakers as newspapers localised their content.

"The local news carved up the states of the Indian union, which made up the Hindi belt; into mappings imposed by the way newspapers evolved their local pages and editions. This had implications for politicians, administrators and social workers and activists working in villages and small towns on various issues," observed Ninan.

By 2005 new modes of financing had come in because of changes in government policy and the Hindi media became its immediate beneficiary with at least one of them the *Dainik Jagran*, acquiring a foreign equity partner. The newspaper was also listed on the stock exchange in 2006.

According to the latest round of the Indian Readership Survey (IRS), *Dainik Jagran* with a certified print audience of 54.5 million is now the most read newspaper in India with another Hindi daily *Dainik Bhaskar* at second place with a readership of 33.5 million. According to the IRS there are as many as four Hindi language newspapers in the top ten list of most read newspapers: *Dainik Jagran*, *Dainik Bhaskar*, *Amar Ujala* and *Hindustan*.

The only English language newspaper in the top fifteen dailies is *The Times of India* which ranks a distant eleventh with a readership of 13.9 million. The remaining slots are taken by Tamil, Marathi, Bengali, Malayalam, Telugu and Hindi newspapers.

Nonetheless, mainstream media for most seemingly news hungry Indians today is TV. In a span of fifty years, the growth of television in India has been nothing short of phenomenal. Beginning with equipment gifted from a foreign government, a makeshift studio and a clutch of 21 television sets installed in homes of select people, TV now has an estimated viewing population of around 600 million, or half the population of the country, whose eyeballs are dispersed across nearly 400 channels, with 211 among them news channels at last country. The whole of Europe in contrast has about 160 news channels.

Despite the slowdown of 2009 caused by the global credit squeeze, there is a huge global buzz about the Indian TV business,

Passengers waiting for trains at Secunderabad station listening to the Railway Budget being presented in the Parliament.

The busy news room of a private news channel of India.

the latest entrant being Turner Asia Pacific Ventures (a subsidiary of Time Warner) buying a 76 per cent stake IDTD Imagine for a total transaction of Rs 585 crore (USD 117 million). Earlier, Scripps Networks of the US had bought 69 per cent stake in NDTV Lifestyle, with entertainment and lifestyle content in the media becoming a major revenue earner across all media platforms. "Television news is arguably the most definitive aspect of modern India's growth in the last decade," says Barkha Dutt, group editor (English News) NDTV and probably the most recognisable India television news personality. "When I joined television in 1994, there were no private television channels in India. The first generation of television journalists in India, were thus, maverick, adventurous risk takers. Over the years, television had to tackle print snobbery and viewer scepticism before it was taken seriously. But over the years it has acquired the power to change mindsets, create moods, alter opinions and bring a frightening level of scrutiny — both good and bad to the reporter on the ground."

After the TV explosion, the third phase of media growth has been powered by the so-called New Media. Slowly, but steadily, the Internet is spreading across the country on the back of high-speed communication lines. Newspaper websites too seem to be making hay out of it. The web editions of Indian newspapers are now read even in smaller towns, and not just in the metros of the country, and are maintained round the clock.

The growth of online newspapers, including in regional languages, in India has been possible due to penetration of computers and easier availability of Internet connections even in small towns. By 2015, Internet penetration is expected to grow to 21 per cent annually from the current 11 per cent.

While Internet user growth has been stymied due to comparatively slower growth of broadband connectivity in the hinterland (this is sought to be rectified by a new policy push by Prime Minister Manmohan Singh), there are no such problems for the mobile phone market. Although mobile internet penetration is just a small fraction of the total user base, service providers have

already begun to offer news through the SMS route. These include news, stock markets, cricket and health. News is the second most popular service amongst mobile users after cricket and is one of the highest revenue earners for SMS content providers.

A potential growth area for mobile news delivery is in the audio segment that can be potentially accessed by a neo-literate population that may not be able to read or write. A pilot project to reach rural populations through mobile handsets is currently under

A woman lights a candle at a candlelight vigil which having been highlighted by an assertive media has become contemporary India's way of voicing its concerns.

way in Sitapur district of Uttar Pradesh through a project being undertaken by the International Media Institute of India (IMII) in partnership with a local NGO.

Radio too has shown a significant resurgence. Once a government monopoly, private and community radio stations have been allowed after the government relaxed its policies and permitted

privatisation, and private radio stations are set to enter the news segment in a controlled manner.

FM radio has driven this explosion in reach — from 76 million individuals listening during an average week in 2005 to as many as 119 million individuals in 2006, a 55 per cent increase during that year and increase of over a 100 per cent from 2002. There are presently 241 FM radio stations spread across 83 cities with

the government planning to further expand FM radio to other cities through private agencies

"India, in terms of what it can do with radio, has enormous potential," says Martin Bowley, a Britain-based expert on the media. "I believe India has the largest untapped market in the world. The potential to advertise through radio is exponential. The rate at which India is growing, radio should command an advertising market share of 10 – 12 per cent soon."

The Federation of Indian Chambers of Commerce and Industry (FICCI) and consultancy firm Price Waterhouse Coopers (PWC) have estimated the current revenues of the radio industry in India at USD 65 million. They have projected that India's radio industry will post a growth of 32 per cent per year over the coming years to touch nearly USD 270 million in revenues by 2010 and require 1.5 million hours of programming every year.

Magazines — even though 2009 has been a bad year with every single of the top twenty-five English magazines registering a drop in circulation — are also expected to grow 11 per cent each year for the next five years making the Indian publishing market an attractive proposition for overseas magazine brands who have been entering into strategic tie-ups with Indian publishing houses to tap niche markets.

All media research points to increased media consumption among consumers from all walks of life. The average Indian, as he becomes aware of India's rising stock in the world and the need to be empowered in an expanding economy, feels a compelling need to be well informed about things, both inside and outside the country. 24X7 news channels provide non-stop information on video terminals in homes, airports, shopping malls, railways stations and public transport.

The sudden growth has also its own set of problems with media explosion not keeping pace with the talent supply. Media schools have mushroomed to provide the industry with reporters,

A woman sips the news of the day at a modern mall in Koramangala in Bangaluru.

editors, and other content writers. More and more younger journalists are finding the industry attractive and are drawn to it by their higher salaries (especially in TV), greater visibility, higher glamour quotient and the sheer thrill of always having the front row seat to the action.

It has also led to an exponential demand for quality content resulting in India having the largest number of news agencies in the world. Besides the PTI and the United News of India (UNI), that have been in existence for decades as they grew under the benign patronage of a government as agencies of record, the media boom has seen the emergence of private news agency players like the Indo-Asian News Service (IANS) and the Asian News International (ANI) to fill the gap in content demand. IANS, particularly, has carved a new trail in Indian news agency journalism by taking the Indian story to many corners of the world and also bringing the Indian story to India from countries and regions from where Indian-interest news was rarely reported before.

However, no story on the Indian media will be complete without a reference to a group of women from Uttar Pradesh whose fortnightly newspaper *Khabar Lahariya* (News Waves) goes to 200 villages and represents the best in India's journalistic courage and ethics. Meera, Shanti, Kavita, Mithilesh, ordinary women from the Chitrakoot and Banda districts in the heart of India's most populous state (166 million, according to the 2001 census), are award-winning journalists, whose newspaper in the local Bundeli language has broken stories, pinned the administration on varied issues and presented a mirror to the society on gender, health and other issues. The behind-the-headlines story of the eight-page newspaper brought out by the group of Dalit women and the behind-the-scenes look at their lives have also been effectively captured in the short film *Taza Khabar - Hot Off The Press* by Delhi-based filmmaker Bishakha Dutta. In March 2004, the women behind *Khabar Lahariya* received the prestigious Chameli Devi Jain award for outstanding mediapersons given by the Media Foundation. "After we won the award, my family members became more supportive," said Shanti. "We give breaking news. Our news makes impact. One of the managers who used to cheat while distributing pension to the

widows was sacked after we published reports against him." Though the reporters themselves market the paper, they have expanded the circulation by hiring agents too, and copies are now available at small shops and tea stalls in even remote villages. Encouraged at receiving the UNESCO's King Sejong Literacy Prize in 2009, Nirantar is now planing to expand *Khabar Lahariya* in Bihar. "The idea of empowering rural women through the medium of newspapers is now spreading," says Shalini Joshi of Nirantar.

Such fascinating media growth stories were narrated at the annual event of the World Association of Newspapers and News Publishers (WAN-IFRA) that took place for the first time in India in the southern city of Hyderabad in late November. The event was a tribute to not just the media freedom in the world's largest democracy, but to a country where the industry has been sustaining extraordinary growth due to the presence of a solid bandwidth of

An old man glancing through a newspaper at a roadside tea stall buzzing with activity in New Delhi.

media professionals who are reinventing every news medium to keep them vibrant and compelling in keeping with the requirements of the digital age.

Tarun Basu is Chief Editor of IANS news agency.

The booming Indian media industry has got everybody excited, even a sadhu who would sit with a copy of a local daily on the ghats of Varanasi to update himself with the affairs of the day.

Passengers buy newspapers at a railway station in Guwahati, Assam.

The Ascent to Modernity

L.K. Sharma

Writer Amitav Ghosh says the intellectual atmosphere in Delhi University is a cut above that at Oxford. Prof David Baltimore, America's Nobel Prize-winning biologist, is surprised by the sheer number of eager young men and women mobbing him at his scientific lectures in Indian cities. The civilisation's appetite for ideas, its perennial character, may have something to do with India's emergence as a knowledge economy and a global technology player. The people's thirst for education has certainly led to the explosive growth of the world's third largest education system.

This system built up after Independence, its serious shortcomings notwithstanding, did propel India into the select nuclear and space clubs. This was achieved largely by India's home-grown scientific and technical manpower that also proved to be crucial for the development of a formidable indigenous manufacturing industry. A country that at the time of its Independence manufactured little of significance, except textiles, went on within a few years to master complex technologies and build space launchers and satellites, super computers, centrifuges and maraging steel.

The creation of a large human resource pool is central to the incredible story of India's development decades. Two generations of doctors, engineers and professionals were nurtured by three generations of teachers — some famed and many unnamed — to shape the India of today. The transition from an agrarian society to an industrial and technological nation took place within ecology of knowledge, culture and creativity. In the realm of fundamental research, India is now invited to join international mega science projects as a valued participant.

A man busy on his mobile phone in front of a billboard featuring Hindu god
Ganesha holding modern technical equipments in Frankfurt, Germany.

India's education system won global recognition for the quality of its select products. Indian doctors formed the backbone of Britain's National Health Service. India trained experts established aided projects in several developing countries. In the course of just a few decades, the higher education institutions bred a significant number of professionals who went on to make an immense contribution to America's intellectual and financial resources. Indian scientists, scholars, economists, engineers, management experts and teachers have risen to eminence in the US. The graduates of India's management institutes today run American banks, investment companies and consultancy firms. The US information technology industry turned the spotlight on Indian technical education. Any new American company, if associated with an Indian name, attracts venture capitalists more easily, so good is the reputation of professional Indians now.

The Indian Institute of Technology (IIT) graduates in

high-tech companies of Silicon Valley and Indian scientists manning NASA are the poster boys of India's education system. Some 40,000 IITians who migrated to the US over the years are credited with creating 150,000 jobs and 80 billion dollars in market capitalisation. Jawaharlal Nehru had envisioned that the IITs would produce the leaders of tomorrow. They did — not just India's, but also of the world!

It is a symbolic throwback to the days when Indian Buddhist scholars from the universities of Taxila and Nalanda traversed distant kingdoms with ideas and ideals. Or to an even earlier period marked by the pre-eminence of Indian astronomers, mathematicians, logicians and philosophers. Then came a time when foreigners arrived in India to gather its spices and pearls. An odd Englishman, wanting to make sense of the exotic, paid respects to India's intellectual heritage by learning at the feet of a Sanskrit pundit. But that was limited to *oriental* learning.

The modern version of this tale is different. Indians now contribute to the fields as varied as string theory, radio astronomy, superconductivity, supercomputers and search engines. India's lunar exploration and a fast breeder reactor are at the cutting edge of the global knowledge system. Then there have been simple but significant innovations such as an inexpensive heart valve, or the Jaipur foot devised by an orthopaedic surgeon that has helped thousands of disabled persons in India and other countries.

India's profile as a commissioned research centre has also changed. Far from being involved in parts of processes and products configured in a distant land, Indian researchers are initiating projects from scratch. *Gurukul*s have been replaced by laboratories and Vedic chants by the whir of computers. Prospectors are now coming in not for spices and gold but to mine the Indian mind in the disciplines hitherto dominated by the West. As aging and other problems shrink Europe's own talent pool for innovation, it turns towards a youthful India.

A hot pursuit of India's intellectual wealth is on. The number of foreign companies with major R&D facilities in India has crossed 400. These are working in various sectors and many have tie ups with Indian companies and higher research institutions. An example of Indian capability is the Indian R&D centres of the Bell Laboratories filing more patents than the US units. The multinationals have been joined by the returning non-resident Indian researchers and entrepreneurs. India is a hot spot in the great global talent search. As a research destination, it is next only to China and the US.

How did it all come about? To begin with, there was the Nehruvian vision of a modern scientific nation rooted in civilisational temper. Historically, the

(*facing page*) The acclaim India receives for its sound intellectual fundamentals is the outcome of a training that requires both the availability of resources as well as firm discipline. The shining future of these girls beckons as they leave home for the lessons of the day in Allahabad.

Nobel Prize winner Dr C.V. Raman.

INDIA R&D HUB

Independent India began with a major state sponsored scientific endeavour and four decades later developed into a favoured R&D destination for foreign technology-rich corporations. They have been scrambling for a piece of the innovations cake in the talent-rich India. They are all here. It is easier to compile a list of the Fortune 100 companies that do not have a R&D centre in India.

The last few years have seen some remarkable discoveries:

1. Indian industry, especially the drugs and automobile sectors, discovered that they must innovate or perish. This has led to several innovations. Some Indian drug companies transited from copying to creating drug molecules.

2. The scientific community responded to the slogan "patent and prosper." Some of them even left public sector laboratories to start their own technology-intensive ventures.

3. Foreign multinationals discovered the intellectual infrastructure of India and established big R&D facilities in this country. Indian companies took up contract research from foreign clients.

4. NRI scientists and technopreneurs discovered a new India where they could live and do business, thus starting the reverse brain drain.

In these new developments, some saw India becoming a unique intellectual and economic power. As CSIR head, Dr R. A. Mashelkar, spearheaded research towards technology development, promoting the concept of "Mind to Market" and an innovation-friendly ecology.

Texas Instruments was among the first multinationals to have established an R&D centre in India way back in 1985. The location got publicised further when John Welch, as chief operating officer of General Electric, made a major commitment in India, by setting up in Bangalore GE's largest R&D outfit outside the US in 2000. Dazzled by the calibre of the Indian PhDs and engineers, he said India was a developed country as far as its intellectual infrastructure was concerned. "We get the highest intellectual capital per dollar here", said the eminent management guru.

As a global R&D hub, India is evolving constantly. The sectors covered range from chip design to chemicals, plastics, and consumer durables to drugs, telecom and IT. Initially, the centres were engaged mainly in such development that will meet the local product needs. Now most of the R&D centres are doing advanced research that is critical to the company's plans in the more sophisticated home market.

While the R&D operations of the foreign multinationals have a beneficial spillover effect on the national innovation system, Indian researchers have set their sights higher. "Indian IQ for Indian IP" is their slogan.

Then there are scientists such as R. A. Mashelkar and Samir Brahmachari looking beyond the model of proprietary knowledge for private profit. They want India to contribute to a global knowledge pool for global good, through global funding. Dr Mashelkar sees India becoming a prime knowledge production centre that will also create much needed public goods to help the growing global population suffer less and live better.

Photocopier drum manufacturing unit Rampur, Uttar Pradesh.

pursuit of knowledge was driven, to a large extent, by intellectual curiosity at the individual level. So also, the country's science and technology plans were driven by the aspiration for development rather than military or commercial objectives. In recent years, with the tide of economic and cultural globalisation sweeping in, the scenario has changed. Thanks to economic and social transformation, the knowledge industry is no longer an oxymoron or a vulgar concept. In fact, it is celebrated. This change is reflected in the popularity of certain fields of study, allocation of resources, new education plan priorities and an increased emphasis on applied research. The swing from the liberal and the classical to the pragmatic and utilitarian is a fact of our time, whatever its reasons or consequences.

As demands on the education system grow, experts have

been highlighting the problems and warning against complacency. The education system is being tuned to the employment market and manpower requirements. The problem being tackled at the official level is one of unequal access. The potential for access remains huge, as the percentage of enrolment in higher education is still pitifully low. More than 100 lakh students enrolled in higher education, represent only 10 per cent of school leavers. The government plans to raise gross enrolment ratio in higher education from 10 to 15 per cent in four years. Such an ambitious venture has encouraged significant private investments in a sector dominated by state-run and state-aided institutions. Private enterprise has already established a major presence in professional education, especially in the engineering and management courses.

The scale of expansion of the demand is visible in the

number of Indian students streaming abroad, as also in the keen interest shown by a host of foreign universities to open shop in India. The reverse traffic too is picking up as more and more overseas students find India an attractive destination. Several premier educational institutions enjoy a good worldwide brand image.

India represents a thriving education bazaar of our time! It produces some 400,000 engineers every year and is far ahead of America in this respect. More software experts work in Bangaluru than in Silicon Valley. All things Indian measure on a mega scale. So, the products that come out of the relatively few islands of excellence in education are indeed huge in numbers. India's higher education system, in scale next only to the US and China, comprises some 400 universities and 18,000 colleges.

The government has ambitious expansion plans covering all streams of learning. It is setting up thirty new central universities, seven IITs and Indian Institutes of Management (IIMs), ten National Institutes of Technology (NIT), five Indian Institutes of Science, Education and Research (IISER), twenty Information Technology Institutes (ITI), two schools of architecture. Educationally backward districts will have more than 300 new colleges. The recent official initiatives also aim at upgrading several institutions.

Research in universities is getting more attention. Steps taken by an empowered committee have increased the numbers of those pursuing doctoral research works in universities and IITs. This will have a significant impact on the country's science and technology system that has till now, drawn its strength mainly from the institutions established to accomplish major scientific missions.

(*Page 181*) School children view the exhibits inside the Science Express at the Jammu railway station. The Science Express, a unique train exhibition specially designed to arouse the curiosity of youth in the field of science and technology, went across fifty-seven cities in India.

(*Page 182*) Tradition holds hands with modernity as these *gurukul* students practice with latest softwares on their computers.

Harvest time in Kuttanadu, Alleppey, Kerala.

The architect of this network, Jawaharlal Nehru, envisioned a nation that pursues scientific knowledge and harnesses it for the good of the people. His commitment stated:

> *It is an inherent obligation of a great country like India, with its traditions of scholarship and original thinking and its great cultural heritage, to participate fully in the march of science, which is probably mankind's greatest enterprise today.*

Nehru established publicly funded laboratories. India was among the first handful of countries to have a minister for science and technology (and still does). As a long-serving Prime Minister, Nehru maintained close contact with eminent scientists and never missed the annual Indian Science Congress Association's session.

With successive Prime Ministers following in his footsteps, India made considerable headway in R&D in the fields of agriculture, space, earth sciences, atomic energy, defence research and biotechnology. These and other programmes have been supported by a huge network of laboratories run by the Council of Industrial and Scientific Research (CSIR), Indian Council of Medical Research (ICMR), Indian Council of Agricultural Research (ICAR), Defence Research and Development Organisation (DRDO), Indian Space Research Organisation (ISRO) and Bhabha Atomic Research Centre (BARC).

Many other prestigious centres of basic and applied research outside this network also command international prestige. These include the Tata Institute of Fundamental Research (TIFR), the Physical Research Laboratory (PRL) and the Indian Institute of Science (IISC). IITs, mainly devoted to teaching, help in specific R&D tasks assigned to them.

When global opportunities beckoned in the field of Information Technology, Indians were ready to compete with the best in the world. Similarly, when the indigenous pharmaceutical industry reached a certain level of competence, resources materialised

GREEN REVOLUTION

A newly independent country wards off mass starvation and predicted famines and becomes the second biggest producer of wheat and an exporter of food grains! This is the story of India's "Green Revolution".

The first signs of the coming Green Revolution appeared in the mid-sixties on the Indian Agricultural Research Institute's (IARI) experimental farms and on the demonstration farms owned by ordinary peasants. From there came glowing reports of successful experiments with the Mexican wheat varieties.

Soon, Dr M. S. Swaminathan, who had led the effort to introduce the high-yielding seeds, came out with a counter prediction: "The wheat harvest of 1968 will mark a new beginning in India's agricultural destiny." It did and Prime Minister Indira Gandhi released in 1968 a special commemorative stamp "The Wheat Revolution".

American scientist Norman Borlaug, whose research in Mexico had paved the way for the Indian Green Revolution, in his Nobel Lecture, applauded the All India Coordinated Wheat Improvement Programme as one of the most extensive and diversified wheat research programmes in the world.

The Green Revolution was the result of agricultural research and technology development matched with adaptation and dissemination through a well-run extension service and public policy package. The semi-dwarf, high-yielding wheat variety seeded the revolution which was carried forward by farmers — young and old, educated and uneducated, who took to the new agronomy. In Punjab, Dr Swaminathan saw, "The divorce between intellect and labour vanishing."

Spectacular harvests set the trend for food sufficiency over the coming decades. Gaining a dramatic (above 30 per cent) improvement in agricultural productivity through the successful introduction of high-yielding seed varieties of wheat, rice, millet and corn, India became an exporter of food grains. India's food grains production went up from 74 million tons in 1966 – 67 to 211 million tons in 2006 – 7. India' wheat production went up from 12 million metric tons in 1965 to 26 million tons in 1972. Rice production went up from 35 million tons in 1972 to 93 million tons in 2002. In the 1960s, rice yields in India were about two tons per hectare; by the mid-1990s, they had risen to six tons per hectare.

As Dr Swaminathan says, during the period 1964 – 68, Indian farmers increased wheat production by a quantity higher than that achieved during the preceding four thousand years, starting from Mohenjodaro. Such a revolutionary progress became possible through the synergy between technology and public policy, supported by farmers' enthusiasm generated through national demonstrations in the fields of small farmers.

The Green Revolution averted impending starvation but it carried some costs. Agricultural scientists had indeed warned of the long-term risks, ranging from an erosion of biodiversity to soil degradation and other ecological ills. With growing concern over the past few years, Dr Swaminathan has been advocating development strategies for ushering in an "Evergreen Revolution."

The issues that surround food production are not of scientific knowledge alone. Who controls science, who finances research and development and who has access to new technologies? The societal context is uppermost in public awareness today, as biotechnology makes further advances.

Dr Swaminathan defines Evergreen Revolution as a revolution that can, "Lead to productuity improvement in perpetuity without associated ecological and social harm." This, according to him, is possible through Green Agriculture involving eco-technologies like integrated pest management, integrated nutrient supply, scientific water harvesting and management and post-harvest management.

for drug research. The biotechnology industry attracted funds as well as scientists and entrepreneurs. Economic liberalisation has made it necessary and profitable for business to venture forth into R&D. Even a traditional industry, such as automobile components, now boasts of a significant R&D effort.

Indian science and technology grew from strength to strength through a process of rising to challenge and overcoming crisis after crisis. The Green Revolution averted a major food crisis through scientific research and farm extension services. In other areas, India's scientific and technical establishment successfully fought off the technology denial regimes designed to crimp its capabilities in sophisticated technologies. A case in point is the denial of super supercomputers and a host of dual use technologies. In the face of technology transfer embargos, India barged into the select club of nuclear powers and space faring nations. It acquired command over the nuclear fuel cycle and high power computing. It established a massive infrastructure to manufacture and launch satellites and to put its space technology to use for rural development. India's pursuit of self-reliance created an ethos in which the nation's scientists held their heads high and confidently charted out ambitious scientific programmes.

India's experience as a space faring nation has been unique. Her first Moon mission and the future plans for planetary explorations are indeed the more dramatic aspects of a space programme that began modestly in the sixties with small sounding rockets. ISRO has taken big strides in space science and technology, simultaneously harnessing these for societal benefits. The satellite communications services were ushered in. The space systems deliver tele-education and telemedicine services. The EDUSAT network has more than 30,000 classrooms connected to academic institutions. More than 230 hospitals and forty-four super speciality hospitals provide health

Doctors in discussion at the Spinal Injury Centre, New Delhi.

care to more than 3,00,000 patients, mostly in the rural areas, through this network. Combining the services offered by a cluster of communication and remote sensing satellites, more than 300 Village Resource Centres (VRC) provide information on natural resources, land and water management, telemedicine, tele-education, health and family planning, vocational training and adult education.

ISRO also conducts basic scientific research, apart from being involved in technology development, space missions and applications in various economic and social sectors. Several of its institutions are known for frontline investigations in the fields of astronomy and atmospheric sciences, using satellites, balloons, sounding rockets and ground-based observatories.

The country's massive infrastructure for space services now boasts of two major operational satellite systems. These are the Indian National Satellite (INSAT) and the Indian Remote Sensing Satellites (IRS). A host of public utility services such as telecommunications, television broadcasting and meteorological services are based on the INSAT series. The successful launch of the state-of-the art remote sensing satellite CARTOSAT-2 in 2007 is providing panchromatic imagery with a resolution of higher than one metre. In the same year, ISRO launched into orbit and recovered a space capsule after performing micro gravity experiments. Such experiments will pave the way for reusable launch vehicles and manned space missions.

Two operational launch vehicles, Polar Satellite Launch Vehicle (PSLV) and Geo-synchronous Satellite Launch Vehicle (GSLV), the first for the polar orbit and the second for the geosynchronous orbit, serve not only the growing requirements of the country but also offer cost-effective launch services for foreign satellites. ISRO's international business arm named ANTRIX has seen the overseas demand for its services growing.

Among the latest achievements of ISRO is the launch of a cluster of ten satellites by a PSLV. The indigenously developed cryogenic upper stage for use in GSLV was successfully ground-tested. It was a technological milestone, as the mastery in this complex field means total self-reliance in the launch vehicle technology. R&D efforts in the areas of semi-cryogenic propulsion stages, air breathing propulsion and reusable launch technology are expected to reduce the cost of space transportation. Infrastructure is being established for developing advanced heavy launchers involving large boosters, liquid propellant engines and cryo boosters.

The space scientists built up indigenous capabilities in the face of limited cooperation by the *space haves* because of strategic and commercial reasons. The nuclear scientists were similarly constrained by the technology denial regimes run by the *nuclear haves*. However, through their relentless progress, India's atomic scientists and engineers brought about a change in the attitude of the US, the leader of all denial regimes. The Bush administration had to recognise India as a country with advanced nuclear technology.

India's advance in the field of atomic energy has fulfilled Dr Homi Bhabha's vision. He, with Nehru's support, gave India an early start. In the forties, he said that when the field of nuclear power develops, India should have her human resources ready. That is what happened. India went on to master the complete nuclear fuel cycle and heavy water production. She has been running nuclear power reactors, refining the fast breeder technology, developing a miniature reactor for submarines, and continuing basic research with applications in diverse fields including defence.

India can boast of a world class capability in the Pressurised Heavy Water Reactor (PHWR) technology. She has operated a small fast breeder reactor since 1985 and is constructing a prototype fast breeder reactor with the capacity of 500 MWe as a commercial demonstrator. When the technology matures, India will be among the leaders in the field. India's unique strategy to meet her future power needs is based on her large deposits of thorium. She will construct a 300 MWe Advanced Heavy Water Reactor (AHWR) which will produce two-thirds of her energy output from thorium.

Nuclear fusion as a source of energy to be supplied by the power companies has been the scientists' dream for long. India's research at home and her participation in the International

India's maiden lunar mission Chandrayaan-1, successfully takes off at the Satish Dhawan Space Centre in Sriharikota, about 100 kilometers north of Chennai.

(*Pages 189 – 190*) Engineers at work at a car manufacturing plant in Pune.

Thermo-nuclear Experimental Reactor (ITER) will ensure that when a breakthrough comes, India does not stand watching from the wings.

Unlike atomic energy, space and defence research that needed massive public funding and the government's direct participation in R&D, in the areas of biotechnology, drug research, information technology, and automobile components it is the private sector that has taken a leading role and won global attention.

India is moving forward in the new and exciting field of nanoscience and technology, with applications in the areas of medicine, electronics and material science. The government drew up a research plan in 2003 and subsequently decided to launch a nano mission with an investment of about Rs 1000 crores for five years. The institutes that will play a key role in this field include the

IISC, the Jawaharlal Nehru Centre for Advanced Scientific Research (JNCASR), the IITs in Mumbai, Delhi and Kharagpur and a couple of CSIR laboratories. *Nano clusters* will be established nationwide to develop applications in diverse sectors. This is being backed by a number of educational projects for training in nanoscience and technology. More than 100 pharmaceutical, biotechnology and biomedical companies have been working on nano-based technologies but the effort is still on a modest scale.

The government is aware of the convergence of nanotechnology with biotechnology and of biotechnology with information technology. Early initiatives by the government to promote biotechnology R&D have yielded significant results. Indian drug industry became a big player in the world's generic drugs market. It has been making a significant proportion of vaccines for the developing world. India has demonstrated her capabilities in

recombinant technology, providing a winning combination of high technology and low costs.

Life sciences have generated stories of innovations and patented processes and products. A large number of scientists emerged as entrepreneurs. Many of them, like the Indian engineers who started their own IT companies, gave up lucrative jobs in the US to start research and development work in India. Observers saw a second wave of biotech entrepreneurship during 2005 – 2006 when over two dozen companies were started up here.

The biotechnology industry is expected to continue to grow between 25 and 40 per cent and reach revenues of 5 billion dollars by 2010 and 25 billion dollars by 2015, according to a BioSpectrum-ABLE Industry Survey. In the field of human genome research, CSIR undertook a unique Indian Genome Variation initiative,

involving 150 participants from diverse disciplines of life sciences, anthropology, statistics and computational biology. An Indian genetic map is expected to provide the base for generating extensive phramacogenomics data that could eventually feed into medical prescriptions, the objective being administration of personalised medicine at an affordable cost.

The biotech entrepreneurs, inspired by the Indian information technology industry, say: "IT today, BT tomorrow." The 60 billion dollar Indian information technology industry had a major influence on the way India was being perceived at one time. Beginning as a service industry propelled by inexpensive skilled manpower, it demonstrated an innovative approach in perfecting an offshore outsourcing model that attracted customers worldwide. It is expected to go on to generate innovative products, both for the domestic and foreign markets. In its current phase of

WHIZ KID NURSERIES

At midnight, after checking into a hotel in the Swedish town of Goteberg, a sleepy Raj Mashruwala is woken up by the receptionist's question. "Are you from the Indian Institute of Technology?" Mashruwala, an alumnus of IIT Bombay, asks the receptionist how does he know the name of IIT? He says he saw the CBS TV news segment *60 Minutes*. This positive account of the IITians was titled 'Imported from India'. "You guys are amazing," he goes on to say. That makes Mashruwala's day!

These products of the premier technical education system of India were part of the force that ushered in the information revolution. The perception of India and Indians changed dramatically after the personal computer revolution and the subsequent dotcom boom of the nineties. Shashi Tharoor says that to the American mind, the stereotypical Indian is no longer a snake charmer but a software guru.

The US, which attracted the IIT graduates in bulk, continues to draw the whiz kids of India. There they have earned name, fame and wealth. *Fortune* took note of them in 2000 as 'The Indians of Silicon Valley', as starters of several successful start-up companies. It was no mean feat for an IITian to be featured as "Asok", one of the characters in the famous cartoon strip, *Dilbert*!

An IITian becomes the head of the Bell Laboratories and is invited to the White House by the US President to receive the National Medal of Technology. The US House of Representatives adopts a resolution to recognise the contribution of the IITs

to America. Bill Gates does not miss a chance to address a gathering of thousands of IITians in the US.

They are running US corporations across sectors, nurturing innovative enterprises or researching in national laboratories. Their own companies have created millions of jobs. Their combined net worth is estimated at 30 billion dollars. What is more important, some of their innovations impacted on the way Americans live. Here the cases of high definition TV and Internet streaming videos and mobile telephony are cited.

The origin of the much acclaimed IIT system lies in the vision of Jawaharlal Nehru who saw science as a modernising force. He was convinced that given the opportunity, millions of Indians would become eminent scientists, educationists, technicians, industrialists — helping to build a new India and a new world. At IIT Kharagpur, Nehru saw it as a fine monument of India, representing her urges and her future in the making. "The picture seems to me symbolic of the changes that are coming to India."

By 1963, the first five IITs — Kharagpur, Bombay, Madras, Kanpur and Delhi — had been established. Two more — Guwahati and Roorkee — were established later. Nine more IITs will be added to these seven. When it comes to admission to the IITs, nothing but merit counts. Through a common admission process, only about 4000 applicants qualify for admission every year, out of more than 1,70,000 students who take the initial screening test. These autonomous institutes of national importance will ensure that the exacting standards are not lowered and the IIT brand is not diluted.

Executives at work in a BPO in New Delhi.

growth, it has the resources, opportunities as well as the need for driving innovations. With her considerable capabilities in the fields of biotechnology and IT, India is destined to become a leader in bioinformatics.

The Indian intellectual fundamentals have always been strong and now new factors have come into play to promote science and technology. The cultural change is narrowing the gap between the mind and the market. Indian scientists are no longer satisfied with publishing papers. The government is increasing the S&T funding and businesses are undertaking R&D in a big way. An innovation movement has begun in India. Having missed the industrial revolution, India is determined to see that it fully participates in the ongoing knowledge-industrial revolution.

L.K. Sharma is Editor of *Innovative India Rises*.

Wind electric farm behind royal cenotaphs, Jaisalmer.

What India Means to Me

India means everything to me. I have no existence without it. I was born here, I grew up here, I make my livelihood here. My sources of inspiration, motivation and concern are all here. The reasons and causes of my despair are also here. My thinking has been shaped by India. It has been the springboard of my imagination. Its complexities and contradictions are as much part of me as I am part of it. I am a composite of its many cultural streams.

I can leave India but India will not leave me.

— Shyam Benegal, Film Director

An idea, a concept, a mood, the smell of wood, smoke at dusk. A land of rhythm that forms the background for Kathak, Odissi, Manipuri, Bharatanatyam, Kathakali. The line of an arm, the curve of a hip, the flash of the eye in *abhinaya*, separately and together.
The beat of *pungcholam* drumming juxtaposed with *chenda* players of Kerala, the magic of the *mridangam* against the *ghatam*, the tantalising tabla taking off on a journey of its own.

Family, spirituality, a coming home. That's India for me.

— Astad Deboo, Dancer.

A soul has no nationality, no religion! Rather I would say that it has only the religion and the nationality of its past lives. Each soul has a history and belongs to some country, some race, where it reincarnates again and again. I consider India as my country, not because I happen to live here, but because the moment I set foot in this country, something deep in me recognised that it was my place, my known territory. Now it is also true that I cannot deny my own culture and upbringing — and I am proud of it in many ways: it allows me to express myself, it gave me the backbone of my professional and literary achievements.

— Francois Gautier, Journalist and Author

When I think of India, I think of steaming breakfast idlis and pungent coconut chutney, of lissom women in saris — the colours of paradise, of the throngs of working men pouring from a brown-and-ochre train. I hear the murmur of the white-specked blue ocean lapping up at sandy beaches, the clear calm stillness of the snow peaks, the cacophony of city traffic, the roar of cheering crowds at a cricket match. I imagine the sun shining off the marble and stone of our greatest monuments, the rain falling vigorous and life-renewing upon the drying plains, the breeze stirring the green stalks of the paddy fields in my village. I remember how, each time that I come home, I stand in the sun and feel myself whole again in my own skin.

— Shashi Tharoor, Author

India represents to me the daring flight of the human spirit trying to manifest the divinity in man through all movements and expressions of life. An old civilisation, the largest democracy of the world comprising of the most diverse ethnic groups, religions, customs, languages, philosophical systems, arts and sciences which has the marvellous faculty of combining the traditional with the most modern. India embodies a stupendous life energy that has survived foreign dominations down the ages, absorbed their influences and tried to find a synthesis by giving her own touch; thus keeping alive her inner unity within this outward diversity.

— Gauri Blomeyer, a child of 'The Mother', Sri Aurobindo Ashram

Foremost she means home for me, my constant point of reference, both defining me and helping me to find myself. She is where I look for meaning, for understanding and for reassurance. She is generous in her affection, welcoming and warm, even in winter. She seems very familiar at times, completely strange at others. At times I am deliriously proud to be Indian, devastatingly ashamed at others; ever so often, her beaten and broken face makes me very sad and angry. She means everything to me and yet is quite beyond me. I cannot disown her, nor can I be at peace with her. She will remain the most exasperating and yet the most precious relation I have.

— Meenaxi Barkotoki, Author and Translator

To be Indian, is to be me. There is no distance. No separation between the two. Identity is such a delicate emotion. The idea of 'Indianness' itself is strangely poignant. It conjures up feelings that are frequently contradictory. Most of us 'feel' Indian…even if our outward lives send out another image. That is the challenge and charm of being Indian. For India touches you in ways that are overwhelming…just as the country itself is. Everything about India is exaggerated…particularly the manner in which we express ourselves. As a writer who has chronicled change for over thirty years in this bewildering country of ours, I have been entirely captivated by her myriad facets and facades. But it is the language of India that I obsess over — language, in the singular. For, even though we have countless 'official' languages and innumerable dialects, we actually

Before the start of every cricket match, he prays for India's victory!

I'm booking you for jumping the red light and over-speeding!
Show me your driving license, registration and insurance papers!

communicate in one language, that too, in such a unique and endearing fashion, the words themselves become unimportant. We speak 'Indian'. This is the warm embrace India extends even to strangers. It is creativity at its most ingenuous. I cherish it, like I do every little aspect of our complex culture. I love India with all its eccentricities and quirks. India is 'Ma'. As simple as that.

— Shobhaa De, Author

When I arrived in India in 1973 as a teacher of German language, I intended to remain just a year or two. I am still here! Why? I am opposed to orientalist notions of an incredible and mysterious India. Rather, I have enjoyed the informality and warmth of the Indian people I have lived with. They exercise a direct emotional appeal to me. I find it challenging as well as refreshing to interact with the rural population among which I stay. My deep respect and love for Rabindranath Tagore and Sri Ramakrishna — who I translate into German — are but extensions of that direct appeal.

—Martin Kampchen, Author and Translator

'What India means to me' is a very strange question, the spontaneous answer to it means a lot to me. In my own identity I experience her history, her trials and tribulations, conflicts and contradictions. In the expanse and range of my multicultural experience of India I traverse/cover her geography. In her arts, dance and music, I assimilate the colours and rhythms of life. Culturally I am fragmented, absorbing, negotiating and mediating with many streams, alienated and rooted both at the same time. In her social inequality I perceive/connect with my innermost guilt and failures as well as desires for a more just world. In her poverty I feel ashamed of my own affluence and yet in her I also derive the relentless spirit to fight to change things. India for me is also a dream, a dream for her people. In essence what India means to me is who I am and who I am becoming.

— Abhilasha Kumari, Sociologist and expert in mass communication studies

I don't know what it means to be an Indian, other than that I have an Indian passport and must give my biometric data to travel to the West. I don't know if I'm proud to be the inheritor of an ancient culture. Cultures aren't wine, they're not necessarily the better for being older. I've never thought too much about being an Indian, because I've never cared much for borders. But India is where I can live and move without a travel document. That's why I'm thankful for India's multiple languages, religions, lifestyles and ethnicities — I'm happy to belong to so many countries.

— Anushka Ravishankar, Author

For almost half a century I have visited India frequently and have lived several years there, I have always felt at home in India and I fondly remember meeting many friendly Indians. Foreigners told me that Indians are arrogant, but in all those years I have never met an arrogant Indian. Arrogance is a reflection of personal tensions. Friendly communication helps to avoid such tensions. Indians can solve many problems by improvisation. If one adjusts to this way of doing things one can get along very well in India. I have learned much in India and this has enriched my life.

— Dietmar Rothermund, India Scholar

Bombay (now Mumbai) has always been one of the cities of my dreams. Karma was on my side, when after being inspired by watching Riyad Wadia's wonderful documentary on his grand aunt *Fearless Nadia*, I was assigned to write a biography on that legendary Indian stunt queen. So I went for the first time in 1996 — and I fell in love with Bombay almost instantly. Never did I go to a place where almost everyone seems more film crazy than I am. Since then, I've never really made it out of the city, even though in total I've not spent more than an year in India. Even if I never saw the Taj Mahal, I've found the city of my dreams.

— Dorothee Wenner, Film-maker

As a first generation Indian-American, I see India more as a 'tossed salad' rather than as a 'melting pot'.

— Mallika Gupta, first generation Indian-American middle class woman living and working in NYC

My last visit to India was in 1992 (aged ten). My mother and I used to visit my grandparents at their house in New Delhi every year until my grandfather died in 1992. My grandmother returned to the UK in the same year and still misses India dreadfully. My grandfather, Enver Ahmed, was a well-known political cartoonist in India and I remember sitting in his study watching him work on cartoon strips that would appear daily in the *Hindustan Times*. My impressions of India, however, are mainly based on the memories of my mother and grandmother. It seems to have been a happy place for them and I look forward to visiting again after so many years, to build my own memories.

— Husna Ahmed, First generation Indian-British woman lawyer, presently living and working in London.

A mostly successful balancing of amazingly diverse attributes is what my country stands for. So India to me means a plethora of festivals celebrated happily with friends of different faiths. It means a diversity of topographies, climates, ethnicities, dress, cuisines, music, literatures, that add up to a rich, vibrant, thriving and always intriguing culture. It means an inspiring history, a promising future, and an energetic present. India is often exasperating and we are still mostly clueless about crisis management, public hygiene or tackling corruption. But India is also the place where a billion plus people can, and do, freely air their opinions on anything under the sun.

India, the concept, is an experiment that many thought was doomed to fail. But even the most cynical admit that today, it is finally on the way to becoming a success story. True, the country is sometimes hiccupping forward rather than galloping ahead. But every hard-won inch is valuable progress in a land as gloriously heterogeneous as ours.

— Mitra Phukan, Author and Singer

I grew up in India and plan to return after living abroad for almost three decades. Having worked most of my life, in the US and globally, on women's rights; I, like feminists from around the world, have always been inspired by the work that women activists in India, such as Ela Bhatt, Renana Jhabvala, Vandana Shiva, Ruth Manorama and so many others — leaders in the global struggle for gender justice have been engaged in. For me, these outstanding women's rights activists represent what India means to me. It is the vibrancy of their activism that compels me to return home.

— Jael Silliman, Feminist and Scholar.

...My e-mail ID is babaji2009@gmail.com!

Glossary

adhunik, p 4, Modern, in this context modern Bangla songs.

al (*Morinda citrifolia*), p 50, The roots of this tree are used as a red dye.

Chamba *rumal*, p 58, An embroidery form influenced by the miniature painting tradition of the region.

charkha, p 50, A hand operated spinning wheel. Mahatma Gandhi brought the *charkha* at centre stage as a symbol freedom and self-reliance during India's Independence movement.

chenda, p 25, A percussion instrument of Kerala used in a Kathakali performance and other traditional theatres.

chikan, p 50, A minute white thread on white muslin embroidery, a specialty of Lucknow, its fine stitches create an embossed and shadowy effect.

chiks, p 50, Window and door blinds made of *sarkhanda* grass bound with cotton thread so that they can be easily rolled up.

chortens, p 4, Trans-Himalayan name for *stupas*, which represent the Buddha.

dhokra, p 42, The *cire perdue* / lost wax method of casting ritualistic and utilitarian objects in brass or bell metal. One of the oldest metal casting techniques, only one piece can be cast from a mould, with each subsequent piece requiring a freshly made mould.

dhol, p 25, A percussion instrument which is played with two sticks, popularly used in the folk dance of Punjab, Bhangra.

edakkai, p 25, A percussion instrument from South India.

eri, p 50, A glossy raw silk produced by a silkworm that feeds on the leaves of the castor plant.

fillum, p 10, A popular way of pronouncing the word 'film' in India.

ganjira, p 25, A percussion instrument of South India played with one hand.

ghatam, p 25, Narrow-mouthed earthenware pot used as a percussion instrument in Carnatic music.

gram devatas, p 52, Village deities.

havelis, p 10, A popular term for mansions in North India.

jalebis, p 109, Sweet meat.

jee, p 9, A way of addressing someone.

kauna, p 50, Local reed growing in the marshes and stagnant waters of Manipur.

kora, p 50, Sedge grass.

kundan, p 55, A method of gem setting over a layer of gold foil set within a gold frame.

lehnga, p 10, A typical Indian dress for girls and women, worn especially on occasions.

lotas, p 52, The versatile pot, in metal or clay, used for ritual and everyday use, its basic shape a throwback to that of a gourd.

maddalam, p 25, A percussion instrument, played with the help of both the palms.

malai, p 107, Milk cream.

masland, p 50, Mats made from a local grass called *madur kathi* i.e. *Cyperus corymbosus*.

melas, p 56, Fairs centred on festivities that mark historical events, mythological heroes, festivals, divine feats, solar or lunar eclipse, and thanksgiving for a bountiful crop or for other reasons.

minakari, p 55, An enamel ornamentation technique wherein colored minerals are fused on to metal, usually silver or gold, giving the metal the appearance of jewelled stone inlay.

mridangam, p 25, An indispensable percussion instrument popular in South India.

muga, p 50, A gold hued silk yarn that is a regional specialty. Produced by a silk worm that is fed on a species of laurel.

nargileh, p 4, A pipe which is used for tobacco consumption in the Middle East.

pakhawaj, p 25, A percussion instrument from North India, is used in *dhrupad*.

pulla, p 50, Cannabis grass, locally called shale.

raita, p 91, A preparation of beaten curd with fruits or vegetables.

rangoli, p 58, Ritualistic floor decoration representing auspicious symbols invoking and seeking protection. Also called *Kolam, Alpona, Mandana*.

sanjhi, p 55, Tradition of ritualistic *rangolis*, created using intricate paper stencils as templates, used in the worship of Lord Krishna in Mathura and Vrindavan.

sarkhanda, p 50, A kind of grass used to make fine bamboo splits.

sheetalpati, p 50, Literally 'cool mat' made from the reed *Maranta dichotama*, locally called *murtha*.

Shilp Shastras, p 52, A compilation of ancient Indian texts that deal with rules on religious art.

shishya, p 45, Disciple.

sikki, p 50, Grows in marshy areas, also called golden grass.

sujani, p 50, Tiny running stitches embroidery on layered cotton with figurative motifs. Traditionally a quilting of old cloth by women in Bihar.

thewa, p 55, A technique wherein intricately filigreed patterned gold leaf is fused on to coloured glass, usually red or green in colour.

thukpa, p 4, A Tibetan noodle soup.

tsampa, p 4, Roasted barley flour, a staple diet in Tibet.

veena, p 25, A string instrument.

Photograph Credits

Front Cover: Bijoy Chowdhury
Pg i: Susannah V. Vergau / photos4dreams
Pg ii & iii: Lakshmi Prabhala
Pg iv & v: Prem Kapoor
Pg vi & vii: Amit Pasricha
Pg 2: Divyesh C. Sejpal
Pg 3: Haran Kumar
Pg 5 & 6: Ranjit Oberoi
Pg 8: Hari Menon
Pg 9: Amit Mehra
P 11: Hari Menon
Pg 12: Elishams
Pg 14: Avinash Pasricha
Pg 15 & 16: Avinash Pasricha
Pg 18: Avinash Pasricha
Pg 19 & 20: Avinash Pasricha
Pg 21 & 22: Amit Pasricha
Pg 24: Avinash Pasricha
Pg 26: Hari Menon
Pg 27: Hari Menon
Pg 29: Amit Pasricha
Pg 30: Hari Menon
Pg 31: Avinash Pasricha
Pg 32: Avinash Pasricha
Pg 34: *Love in Ancient India*
Pg 35: Shakuntala Ramani
Pg 36: Shakuntala Ramani
Pg 37: Anamitra Chakladar
Pg 39: Suprabha Nayak (copyright Visual Arts Gallery India Habitat Centre)
Pg 40: Nevil Zaveri
Pg 41: Suprabha Nayak (copyright Visual Arts Gallery India Habitat Centre)
Pg 43 & 44: Amit Pasricha
Pg 46: Divyesh C. Sejpal
Pg 47: Lakshmi Prabhala
Pg 48: Benedicte Martin Verma for Craft Revival Trust
Pg 49: Prem Kapoor
Pg 51 & 52: Prem Kapoor
Pg 53 & 54: left and right photographs – Benedicte Martin Verma for Craft Revival Trust, centre photograph – Diya Dasgupta
Pg 55: Benedicte Martin Verma for Craft Revival Trust
Pg 56: Diya Dasgupta
Pg 57 & 58: Hema Narayanan
Pg 60: Associated Press

Pg 61 & 62: Taken from official movie websites
www.omshantiom.erosentertainment.com (*left*)
www.lagaan.com (*centre*)
www.cc2c-thefilm.com (*right*)
Pg 63 & 64: Dinodia Photos
Pg 65: Susannah V. Vergau / photos4dreams
Pg 66: Susannah V. Vergau / photos4dreams
Pg 68: Vivek M
Pg 69 & 70: Ranjit Oberoi
Pg 70 (top): *The Hindu*
Pg 71 & 72: *The Legends of Indian Cinema*
Pg 74: Ranjit Oberoi
Pg 75: Amit Pasricha
Pg 76: Associated Press
Pg 77: Hemant Mehta/IndiaPicture
Pg 79: Anja Cronenberg
Pg 80: Ranjit Oberoi
Pg 81 & 82: Ranjit Oberoi
Pg 83: Elishams
Pg 84: Divyesh C. Sejpal
Pg 85 & 86: Nevil Zaveri
Pg 88: Phal Girota
Pg 89: Elishams
Pg 90: Ranjit Oberoi
Pg 92: Hari Menon
Pg 93 & 94: Hari Menon
Pg 95: Anja Cronenberg
Pg 96: Deepak's Photocurry
Pg 98: Anamitra Chakladar
Pg 101 & 102: Elishams
Pg 104: Jaybee, Chennai
Pg 105 & 106: amitverma.in
Pg 108: Anuj Parti
Pg 109 & 110: Amit Pasricha
Pg 111 & 112: Amit Pasricha
Pg 114: Amit Pasricha
Pg 116: Associated Press
Pg 117: Associated Press
Pg 118: Associated Press
Pg 119: Associated Press
Pg 120: Gagan Narang from *The Commonwealth Journey*
Pg 121: Associated Press
Pg 122: Associated Press
Pg 123: Associated Press
Pg 124: Associated Press
Pg 125: Associated Press

Pg 126: Associated Press
Pg 128: Photos of Kar
Pg 129: Associated Press
Pg 130: Gagan Narang from *The Commonwealth Journey*
Pg 132: Gagan Narang from *The Commonwealth Journey*
Pg 134: Associated Press
Pg 135: Dinodia Photos
Pg 136: Elishams
Pg 137 & 138: Amit Pasricha
Pg 140: Associated Press
Pg 141: Associated Press
Pg 142: Associated Press
Pg 144: Associated Press
Pg 145 & 146: Ranjit Oberoi
Pg 148: Photos of Kar
Pg 150: Hari Menon
Pg 151: Susannah V. Vergau / photos4dreams
Pg 152: Hari Menon
Pg 154: Associated Press
Pg 155 & 156: Amit Pasricha
Pg 157: Ranjit Oberoi
Pg 159 & 160: Amit Pasricha
Pg 162: Ranjit Oberoi
Pg 163 & 164: Ranjit Oberoi
Pg 165 & 166: Associated Press
Pg 168: *The Hindu*
Pg 169: Associated Press
Pg 170: Associated Press
Pg 171: *The Hindu*
Pg 172: *The Hindu*
Pg 173: Ankur Warikoo
Pg 174: Associated Press
Pg 176: Associated Press
Pg 177: Associated Press
Pg 178: Dinodia Photos
Pg 180: Amit Pasricha
Pg 181: Associated Press
Pg 182: Parmarth Niketan
Pg 183 & 184: Hari Menon
Pg 186: Amit Pasricha
Pg 188: Associated Press
Pg 189 & 190: Amit Pasricha
Pg 192: Amit Pasricha
Pg 193 & 194: Amit Pasricha
Back Cover: Amit Pasricha